HOME ICE

CANADA'S 2010
MEN'S OLYMPIC HOCKEY
TEAM GUIDE

LORNA SCHULTZ NICHOLSON

FOREWORD BY **STEVE YZERMAN** INTRODUCTION BY **BOB NICHOLSON**

Fenn Publishing Company Ltd.
Toronto, Canada

Fenn Publishing Company Ltd.

Home Ice

A Fenn Publishing Book / First Published in 2009

All rights reserved

Text Copyright © Lorna Nicholson

Copyright © Hockey Canada

The publisher gratefully acknowledges the support of the Canada Council for the Arts and the Ontario Arts Council for its publishing program. We acknowledge the support of the Government of Ontario through the Ontario Media Development Corporation's Ontario Book Initiative.

THE CANADA COUNCIL | LE CONSEIL DES ARTS
FOR THE ARTS | DU CANADA
SINCE 1957 | DEPUIS 1957

ONTARIO ARTS COUNCIL
CONSEIL DES ARTS DE L'ONTARIO

We acknowledge the financial support of the Government of Canada through the Book Publishing Industry Development Program (BPIDP) for our publishing activities.

Designed by First Image

Fenn Publishing Company Ltd.
Toronto, Ontario, Canada

Printed in Canada

All photos courtesy of **Hockey Canada**, except those listed below, or noted beside the photo.

Getty Images: 13 [bottom], 17 [top], 21 [top], 25 [bottom], 29 [top], 34, 38,42,45, 51,54, 59, 63, 66, 71, 73, 79, 82, 85, 89, 94, 99, 102, 106, 111, 113,119, 123, 125, 130, 133, 138, 142, 147, 150, 154, 159, 162, 167, 170, 174, 177, 182, 187, 189, 194

Library and Archives Canada Cataloguing in Publication

Schultz Nicholson, Lorna
   Home ice : Canada's 2010 men's olympic hockey team guide / Lorna Schultz Nicholson.
ISBN 978-1-55168-325-6

   1. Hockey—Canada. 2. Hockey players—Canada—Biography.
3. Winter Olympic Games (21st : 2010 : Vancouver, B.C.). I. Title.
GV848.4.C3S36 2009   796.962'66   C2009-902285-0

CANADA

® Registered trademark of Hockey Canada
® Marque déposée de Hockey Canada

Officially licensed product of Hockey Canada.
Produit officiellement licencié de Hockey Canada.

The Team Canada logo is a registered trademark of Hockey Canada and is used under license by Fenn Publishing Company Ltd..

Le logo d'Équipe Canada est une marque déposée de Hockey Canada et utilisée sous licence par Fenn Publishing Company Ltd..

Acknowledgements

I am very grateful that so many people helped me put this book together. Without them the book would not be possible. For insight on the players bios my thanks goes to Ken Hitchcock, Kevin Lowe, Doug Armstrong, Ken Holland, Bob Nicholson and Pierre McGuire. Steve Yzerman was gracious enough to take the time to write a foreword for the book. Andre Brin at Hockey Canada promptly answered my numerous emails on everything and anything, even when he hadn't slept for days because he was organizing the camp. Chris Jurewicz and Paula Lally at Hockey Canada helped me with the management bios. In collecting photos of the players, I had unbelievable help from agents, parents, NHL franchises and hockey personnel: Pat Brisson (agent), Patrick Morris (agent), Gerry Johannson (agent), J.P. Barry (agent), Rick Curran (agent), Judd Moldaver (agent), Dave Branch (OHL), Aaron Bell (OHL), Dan Hamilton (OHL), Gilles Corteau (QMJHL), Sean Kelso (Calgary Flames), Tom Roly (San Jose Sharks), Tim Darling (Nashville Predators), Nate Ewell (Washington Capitals), Phil Legault (Ottawa Senators), Sergey Kocharo (Phoenix Coyotes), TC Carling (Vancouver Canucks), Ruthann Sharp (parent), Sue Carter (parent), Linda Staal (parent), Trina Crosby (parent), Donna Spezza (parent), Laurel Ward (parent), Chris Wojicik (University of Vermont), Andy McDonald (player), Aaron Wilson (Hockey Canada), Kelly Findley (Hockey Canada), Jennifer Robins (Hockey Canada), Bruce Newton (Hockey Canada), Ben Aycock (Carolina Hurricanes), Jason Rademan (Dallas Stars), Mike Caruso (St. Louis Blues), Bruce Hamilton (Kelowna Rockets), Frank Darin (Sherwood Signs, Penticton), Johnny Misley (Hockey Canada).

   Designer Michael Gray of First Image is fantastic at organizing images and text to make everything work well together. And, of course, I have to thank my publisher, Jordan Fenn and the entire team at Fenn Publishing. They are amazing to work with and are always there to support and encourage and… keep me on my deadline.

Lorna Nicholson

CONTENTS

CANADA

BOB NICHOLSON

INTRODUCTION

The depth of our Men's 2010 Olympic Hockey Team surpasses any team that Canada has ever put together. This is a true testament to all the minor hockey programs that are run across Canada. Our 13 branches are doing an unbelievable job of developing players who feed into Hockey Canada's high performance programs. I have always said that our grassroots programs are so important to our elite programs. Since players are being taught how to play the game properly at an early age, we get the results on the world stage that Canadian fans love so much. Our U-17 and U-18 programs have become so successful; they are direct contributors to our World Junior program and our Senior Men's program. When you read this book you will see how many of the players on the roster have played in some capacity for Hockey Canada—and won gold medals—many starting in the U-18 programs or with our World Junior program.

All of the players on this roster are capable of playing with the best in the world. I can honestly say that I feel our players are the most skilled in the world. When they slip on the Hockey Canada jersey, they wear it with pride, and they represent our country both on and off the ice. They make us proud.

We wouldn't be where we are today without the support that goes on behind the scenes. I would like to personally thank all the minor hockey associations and coaches in Canada. Keep up the good work. I know you're passionate about our game, and it shows. The CHL is also a league that continues to work with us on developing players, and they always help support our U-18 and World Junior Team. Moving up the ladder, I also have to thank the NHL teams and owners for allowing us to have your players, and for interrupting your schedule so they can play for Canada. And, of course, how could I even write this introduction without saying a word of thanks to the parents of these wonderful athletes. Yes, I know how much time you have spent at rinks all across Canada.

The key for Hockey Canada with this 2010 Olympic team is to make sure that every stage of the preparation is taken care of. I feel that this is definitely being done by my staff. They don't work nine-to-five, but put in countless hours that go well beyond the normal working day. And of course, our executive director, Steve Yzerman, and our head coach, Mike Babcock, and their respective management teams, have worked extremely hard to prepare the team and make sure that everything is running smoothly at all times.

In closing, I want to say thanks to the athletes. Every one of you deserves to be here, and I really appreciate your time and effort to play for Hockey Canada. I'm looking forward to seeing you win gold on *Home Ice*.

FOREWORD

STEVE YZERMAN

I believe the Canadian Men's 2010 Olympic orientation camp was a success. At this point I can't tell you who will be on the final roster—so much can happen between now and late-December when we make our announcement. What I can tell you, though, is that as a management team, we will be watching all the players closely this fall during the NHL season.

Many people are asking how we are picking the team. What are we looking for in a player? Every player who makes the 2010 Olympic roster will have an important job to do. We want quality and depth at each position so our team has no weaknesses. We intend to be strong in all parts of the game, both at even strength and on special teams.

The reality, however, is that when we start playing in Vancouver, there will be some elite players asked to take on a different role than they're used to. That's just the way the game evolves. To me, each role is important. Just take a look back at the 2009 Stanley Cup Playoffs, game seven in Detroit. Maxime Talbot scored two goals to lead Pittsburgh to victory. Before the game everyone was wondering who the heroes would be. Crosby? Malkin? Datsyuk or Zetterberg? We will need great contributions from all our players regardless of how much, or where, they play.

We're not sure who will play where; plans can change quickly in these tournaments. The coaches will be required to make adjustments quickly in both personnel, and strategy, to ensure success. It will be a very exciting tournament!

From watching the players at the orientation camp, I believe that we're going to have one of the strongest, most competitive teams Canada has ever put together. We have some difficult decisions to make, but we're looking forward to putting together a team that has potential to win gold on home soil!

It's a great honour, and I'm very excited to be a part of the Canadian Men's Olympic Hockey Team.

HOCKEY CANADA MANAGEMENT

BOB NICHOLSON

Hometown: Penticton, British Columbia
Birthdate: May 27, 1953, Vancouver, British Columbia

Hockey Experience: Bob has been Hockey Canada's president since 1998. He has overseen Canada winning 52 medals in international competition since 1990, 33 of which were gold: three that were Olympic Gold medals, (2002–men, 2002–women, 2006–women). He was also the senior vice-president of Hockey Canada from 1992-1998, and has served on several sports advisory committees and the IIHF Coaching Committee. He served as the technical director for the British Columbia Amateur Hockey Association from 1979-1989. He was inducted into the B.C. Hockey Hall of Fame in 2004. Bob played Junior A hockey in Penticton, British Columbia and NCAA hockey at Providence College.

Current Role in Hockey: **President and CEO Hockey Canada**

STEVE YZERMAN

Hometown: Nepean, Ontario
Birthdate: May 9, 1965, Cranbrook, Ontario

Hockey Experience: Steve has served as Canada's general manager at the 2007 and 2008 IIHF World Championships. As a player, he represented Canada eight times: 2002 Winter Olympic Games winning gold, 1998 Winter Olympics, 1996 World Cup of Hockey, 1990 IIHF World Championship, 1989 IIHF World Championship, 1985 IIHF World Championship, 1984 Canada Cup winning the Cup, and 1983 IIHF World Junior Championship. He played for the Detroit Red Wings for 22 seasons before retiring on July 3, 2006. Steve led the Red Wings to three Stanley Cup Championships in 1997, 1998, 2002. He is the longest serving captain of any team in North America, and was inducted into the Hockey Hall of Fame in 2009.

Current Role in Hockey: **Executive Director, Team Canada; Vice President and Alternate Governor of the Detroit Red Wings**

"Participating on the Olympic management team is one of the most humbling, yet exciting, experiences of my professional life. I look forward to the responsibility of helping to create a team that Canada will be proud of!"

DOUG ARMSTRONG

Hometown: Sarnia, Ontario
Birthdate: September 24, 1964

Hockey Experience: Doug was Canada's general manager at the 2009 IIHF World Championship, the assistant general manager at the 2008 IIHF World Championship in Quebec City, a special advisor to general manager Steve Yzerman at the 2007 IIHF World Championship, and he also served as the assistant general manager at the 2002 IIHF World Championship. Doug is the assistant general manager of the St. Louis Blues, and will become general manager at the end of his two-year contract. He spent parts of seven seasons (2002-07) as general manager of the Dallas Stars, and 16 years as part of the Dallas/Minnesota franchise.

Current Role in Hockey: **Associate Director Team Canada; Vice President, Player Personnel St. Louis Blues**

KEN HOLLAND

Hometown: **Vernon, British Columbia**
Birthdate: **November 10, 1955**

Hockey Experience: Ken was Canada's general manager at the 2006 IIHF World Championship and was Canada's assistant general manager at the 2005 IIHF World Championship. Ken played four games in the NHL as a goalie. After he retired from hockey, he spent seven years as the Director of Amateur Scouting for the Detroit Red Wings and three as the assistant general manager. In 1997, he was hired as the general manager of the Detroit Red Wings, and has since won three Stanley Cups (1998, 2002, 2008). He also won a Stanley Cup in 1997 as assistant general manager.

Current Role in Hockey: **Associate Director Team Canada; Executive Vice President, General Manager and Alternate Governor Detroit Red Wings**

"This is a once in a lifetime opportunity! It is an incredible honour to represent my country in the Olympics, in my home province, with Steve Yzerman and the awesome staff he put together. I am very humbled and honoured to be selected to represent Canada."

KEVIN LOWE

Hometown: **Lachute, Quebec**
Birthdate: **April 15, 1959**

Hockey Experience: Kevin was Canada's assistant executive director for the Men's team at the 2006 Winter Olympic Games, the 2004 World Cup team (which won the Cup), and the 2002 Olympic Winter Games (which won the gold medal). He also represented Canada twice as a player, winning the Canada Cup in 1982 and a bronze medal with Canada at the 1982 IIHF World Championship. Kevin played 19 NHL seasons for the Edmonton Oilers and four with the New York Rangers. He won six Stanley Cups, five with the Oilers (1984, 1985, 1987, 1988, 1990), and one with the Rangers (1994).

Current Role in Hockey: **Associate Director Team Canada; President, Hockey Operations Edmonton Oilers**

"Words can't really describe the honour I feel being asked to be a part of the management team for the Canadian Men's Olympic hockey team. Having spent my entire life involved in hockey, all but four of those years in Canada, I know how much hockey means to the people of our country."

MIKE BABCOCK

Hometown: **Saskatoon, Saskatchewan**
Birthdate: **April 29, 1963 in Manitouwadge, Ontario**

Hockey Experience: Mike led Canada's National Men's team to the gold medal at the 2004 IIHF World Championship. He also coached Canada's National Junior Team in the 1997 IIHF World Junior Championship, winning gold. He is the only Canadian coach to have won gold at both the IIHF World Championship and the IIHF World Junior Championship. He played in the WHL and also played for the University of Saskatchewan and McGill University. He coached in the WHL for the Moose Jaw Warriors and the Spokane Chiefs, and also in the AHL with the Cincinnati Mighty Ducks. Then he moved into the NHL, and was the Head Coach for the Anaheim Mighty Ducks before becoming Head Coach of the Detroit Red Wings. He has won one Stanley Cup, in 2007-08, with the Detroit Red Wings.

Current Role in Hockey: **Head Coach Team Canada; Head Coach Detroit Red Wings**

"We have such a great group of talent and it's going to be a great team. We have the environment and the climate that expects success, so we want everyone on our team to lead. We want trust from every player, everywhere in the rink. We are not picking third- and fourth-line players, but players who are trustworthy, which means we are asking players to do things differently."

KEN HITCHCOCK

Hometown: Edmonton, Alberta
Birthdate: December 17, 1951

> "We're going to have the loudest crowd. We're not going to be afraid to win. We're not going to have players who are afraid to win and feel stressed out and pressured. We're just not going to do that pressure stuff. We're going to be ready to play and compete."

Hockey Experience: Ken was Canada's head coach at the 2008 IIHF World Championship, and was an associate coach with Canada at the 2006 Olympic Winter Games and the 2002 IIHF World Championship. As an associate coach, he won the 2004 World Cup of Hockey, a gold medal at the 2002 Olympic Winter Games, and a gold medal with the 1988 IIHF World Junior Championship. Ken Hitchcock coached for six years in the WHL from 1984-1990. In 1990, he moved to the NHL and was assistant coach for the Philadelphia Flyers. Wanting to be a head coach, he moved to the IHL Kalamozoo Wings in 1993-94 season, and was there until he was hired by the Dallas Stars as their head coach in January, 1996. He spent seven years in Dallas and four years back in Philadelphia with the Flyers before he took the job as head coach with the Columbus Blue Jackets.

Current Role in Hockey: **Associate Coach Team Canada; Head Coach Columbus Blue Jackets**

JACQUES LEMAIRE

Hometown: LaSalle, Quebec
Birthdate: September 7, 1945

> "It's something special. I'm toward the end of my career. As a coach, I'm getting closer and closer every year to retiring, then this comes up and it's really exciting. And what's most exciting is the group I will be working with. They're all guys I have admired and I always thought they were top coaches in the league. And to be part of that, you can't ask for more."

Hockey Experience: Jacques Lemaire played his entire hockey career with the Montreal Canadiens, winning the Stanley Cup eight times, (1968, 1969, 1971, 1973, 1976, 1977, 1978, 1979). He retired in 1979 and started his coaching career in Switzerland. From 1983-85 he was the head coach for the Montreal Canadiens, and from 1993-98 he was the head coach for the New Jersey Devils. From 2000-09, he was the head coach for the Minnesota Wild. Jacques has just been rehired by the New Jersey Devils for the 2009–10 season. This marks his first international experience with Canada.

Current Role in Hockey: **Associate Coach Team Canada; Head Coach New Jersey Devils**

LINDY RUFF

Hometown: Warburg, Alberta
Birthdate: February 17, 1960 in Edmonton Alberta

> "I think the way to relieve the pressure is by being prepared. By knowing we've done the work, and we're ready to go. We must approach it that way, and get the players to embrace it. We have to be comfortable with how we're going to play, knowing that there are good players all around the world, and there are good lines out there. We just have to be ready."

Hockey Experience: Lindy played for the Buffalo Sabres for 10 seasons, and also for the New York Rangers for three. From 1993 to 1997, he was the assistant coach for the Florida Panthers. In 1997, he was named the head coach for the Buffalo Sabres. Lindy was Canada's head coach at the 2009 IIHF World Championship in Switzerland, winning a silver medal.

Current Role in Hockey: **Associate Coach Team Canada; Head Coach Buffalo Sabres**

Johnny Misley
Executive Vice President, Hockey, Hockey Canada

Johnny is responsible for providing both leadership and direction for Canada's national teams at World Championships, World Cups, and Olympic and Paralympic Games. He has coached at the minor, Major Junior and international levels for more than 25 years, and played and coached professionally in Italy and Germany between 1985 and 1990.

TEAM SUPPORT

Sr. Director, Men's National Teams: **Brad Pascall** .....

Director, Men's National Teams: **Scott Salmond** ....

Video Manager: **Ben Cooper** ....

Team Doctor: **Dr. Jim Thorne** ....

Equipment manager: **Pierre Gervais** ....

Equipment manager: **Pat O'Neill** ....

Athletic Therapist: **Mike Burnstein** ....

Athletic Therapist: **Jim Ramsey** ....

Therapist: **Kent Kobelka** ....

Media Relations: **Andre Brin** ....

Media Relations: **J.J. Hebert** ....

Coordinator, Men's National Teams: **Mark Black** ....

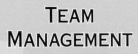

CANADA

LORNA NICHOLSON

INTRODUCTION

This book first originated in a conversation I had with Jordan Fenn (Fenn Publishing) in the winter of 2008, when he was in Calgary for a meeting with Hockey Canada. Initially, I was going to write a book that would highlight the players who were on the final roster for the 2010 Canadian Men's Olympic Team. Then I was in Toronto at a meeting with Jordan, Bob Nicholson (President Hockey Canada), and Scott Smith (Vice-President Hockey Canada), and we started talking about the August orientation camp, and the 46 players who the Hockey Canada management team had picked to be in attendance. They are all fantastic players. That's when we decided that all the players invited to the camp deserved to be recognized, and that Canadian fans would want information on every player so they could debate who they would pick for their final roster.

The August orientation camp was not to pick the team, but a get-together to tell the players about the Olympic Games' procedures.

The camp included three days of on-ice training and ended with a Red and White scrimmage, played at the Saddledome in Calgary. In front of an excited, sold-out crowd, the 46 players put on a spectacular show, proving that Canada could put together two Olympic teams and both would be able to compete internationally. As I watched the entertaining game, I was thrilled that we had decided to highlight all the players at camp. Every single one of them deserved to be recognized. I don't envy the job of the management team as they have to evaluate the 46 players this fall as they play for their respective NHL teams. But the list will have to be shortened. I suspect the final roster will be out in late December. Every Canadian fan will be waiting for that day to see if their favourite player was chosen.

I have been extremely lucky to have attended both the 2002 and 2006 Winter Olympics. The 2002 Salt Lake City Olympics was the ultimate experience as Canada won the gold medal in both men's and women's hockey.

Winning on *Home Ice* would be even more fantastic, especially when all of our hockey teams will be wearing such a unique Canadian jersey. Our new Canadian jersey weaves a story of Canada's abounding history through icons and cultural symbols. The smaller Maple Leafs on the inside of the bigger Maple Leaf represent the gold medal count for our men's, women's and sledge teams; the thunderbird and eagle, two First Nation symbols, are there to support and protect the central Maple Leaf; and the hockey player and stick symbolize the great sport of hockey.

The energy at the orientation camp was electric, positive, and respectful. So get ready to pick your team. Then, get ready to celebrate.

MARTIN BRODEUR

GOALTENDER #30

Catches: **Left**
Height: **6'2"**
Weight: **210 lbs**
Birthdate: **May 6, 1972**
Birthplace: **Montreal, QC**
Hometown: **Montreal, QC**
Team: **New Jersey Devils (NHL)**
MHA: **AMH St-Léonard (QC)**
NHL Draft: **New Jersey Devils: 1990 (1, 20)**
Last Amateur Club: **Lazers de St-Hyacinthe (LHJMQ)**

The job of picking the goalies for an Olympic squad is never easy. The team's management staff gather around a boardroom table for hours—and often days—hashing and re-hashing strengths and weaknesses, experience, playing style, leadership, and trustworthiness when it comes to the critical moments and the big games.

Every person on the Hockey Canada management team knows that Martin Brodeur possesses the required attributes to become the starting netminder for 2010. Firstly, let's look at his experience. Rewind 14 years to 1996 and you will see Martin Brodeur's name on the Hockey Canada rosters for both the World Cup of Hockey and the IIHF (International Ice Hockey Federation) Men's World Championship. Both teams won silver medals in 1996.

Now, let's fast forward six years to Canada's 2002 Olympic gold medal in Salt Lake City and you will see Brodeur's name on the final game sheet as the starting goalie. Brodeur was actually selected as the number two goalie behind Curtis Joseph, though after the first game, that all changed.

Canada first met Sweden and Brodeur took his position on the bench. The game was a frustrating one, that fans and players lost sleep over as Canada came out flat and lost the contest 5-2. The media blasted Team Canada for their lazy play, their horrible start and their lack of urgency. Of course—and for good reason—Canadian hockey fans were irate; this was a team with all the manpower to win and to win big; though so too was our roster at the 1998 Nagano Games and that was of little consequence.

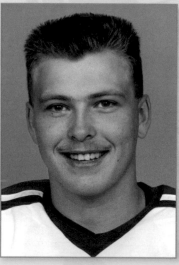

A head shot of Martin Brodeur as a teenager from when he was invited to the 1991 IIHF World Junior Selection Camp.

Martin Brodeur celebrating after winning the gold medal at the 2002 Olympic Games.

Favourite TV show:
Seinfeld

Best concert ever attended:
Metallica

Person who had most influence on hockey career growing up:
Dad

Most memorable minor hockey experience:
playing for Team Quebec in an under-16 tournament

Hockey hero:
Patrick Roy

Favourite book:
Grant Fuhr biography

Charities supported:
Breakfast Club of Quebec

If not a hockey player would be a:
golfer

New Jersey Devils

Martin Brodeur

After a half century without an Olympic gold medal, the expectations placed on our 2002 men's team to reclaim Canada's glory was intense, and no one knew this more than Hockey Canada's coaching and management staff. After the team's dismal performance in game one, Wayne Gretzky as Executive Director, along with head coach Pat Quinn and the rest of the management team, including: Kevin Lowe, Steve Tambellini, Ken Hitchcock, Jacques Martin and Wayne Fleming met and together made difficult, yet important decisions and replaced Joseph with Brodeur for game two.

With Brodeur in net, Canada was undefeated for the remainder of the tournament. Stopping shot after shot, playing his stick well, and his hybrid style of mixing both a stand-up and butterfly style, earned him each victory and it was with a huge smile that he bowed his head after the final game and welcomed the gold medal to be placed around his neck.

Two years later Brodeur was selected as the starting goalie for the 2004 World Cup of Hockey. This team went one step further and had a flawless record to capture the Cup. Brodeur was then selected again as the starting goalie for the 2006 Turin Olympics but after a disappointing team appearance, Brodeur will surely be eager for redemption in Vancouver.

Does Martin Brodeur still have what it takes to be a starting goalie for an Olympic squad? He is the winningest goalie in NHL history, having surpassed Patrick Roy, and he is also close to breaking the all-time shutout record. There is no doubt the coaches and management team will be watching the New Jersey Devils number one goalie in the fall of 2009. During the 2008-09 season, Brodeur was out with injuries and missed more than 40 games. Sometimes, with veteran players, recovery time takes longer, but when Brodeur returned to the ice, he played as if he had never been injured.

The Hockey Canada management team like Brodeur because he has experience; 14 years worth. They like him because he has focus and determination and is known to play well in key games. They like him because of his big-game playoff knowledge and Stanley Cup victories. And they like him because he's the best stand-up goalie in the NHL. This is not an easy style to play, and as a result, many goalies don't even try, but Brodeur has mastered staying on his skates and kicking out his legs to stop the puck, rather than flopping down into a butterfly and making himself vulnerable and out of position to stop a possible rebound. A quick thinker, he is also good with his stick and can move the puck out of the zone fast. This ability is helpful defensively, though contributes equally offensively, as Broduer's many assists demonstrate.

Brodeur gets along with everyone on and off the ice. He is known to talk to the young guys to make them feel comfortable. In practices, he challenges the players in a fun, competitive way. With all of these attributes, Brodeur will definitely be a contender for the number one goalie spot if he stays healthy and injury-free.

August 2009 orientation camp

Camp Highlights

Brodeur played spectacular hockey, giving the sold-out crowd in Calgary a great show. His finest moment was when he snapped the puck out of the air to rob a stunned Jason Spezza of a late first-period goal. This big save gave Brodeur a shutout in the first period, giving him the third star of the game in the Calgary Herald. He had 12 shots on net and made 11 saves.

Statistics– **International**											
Year	Team	Event	GP	MIN	GA	SO	GAA	W-L-T	SOG	SV%	Result
Regional											
1989	QC	U17				unavailable					n/a
National											
1996	CAN	WHC	3	140	9	0	3.43	0-1-1	61	0.869	Silver
1996	CAN	WC	2	60	4	0	4.00	0-1-0	26	0.846	Silver
1998	CAN	OLY	-	-	-	-	-	-	0	0	4th
2002	CAN	OLY	5	300	9	0	1.80	3-1-1	109	0.917	Gold
2004	CAN	WC	5	300	5	1	1.00	5-0-0	129	0.963	1st
2005	CAN	WHC	7	419	20	0	2.87	5-2-0	218	0.901	Silver
2006	CAN	OLY	3	179	6	0	2.01	2-0-1	104	0.923	7th
	CAN	INTL TOTAL	25	1398	53	1	2.24	15-5-2	647	0.918	
	CAN	SR TOTAL	25	1398	53	1	2.24	15-5-2	647	0.918	

Marc-André Fleury

GOALTENDER #29

Catches : Left
Height: 6′2″
Weight: 180 lbs
Birthdate: November 28, 1984
Birthplace: Sorel, QC
Hometown: Sorel, QC
Team: Pittsburgh Penguins (NHL)
MHA: AHM Sorel
NHL Draft: Pittsburgh Penguins: 2003 (1, 1)
Last Amateur Club: Cape Breton Screaming Eagles (QMJHL)

Although from a different generation than Martin Brodeur, (he is 12 years younger and lists his hockey idols as Martin Brodeur and Patrick Roy), Marc-André Fleury has racked up some significant championship victories. Having playoff experience and big-game success always helps a player's chances when the final roster for the Olympic team is being selected.

This young goalie earned his way to orientation camp by playing as the starting goalie for the 2009 Stanley Cup Champions. Some key saves for the Pittsburgh Penguins in the final series against the highly-skilled Detroit Red Wings made the Hockey Canada management staff take a good, long look at this Quebec born player and they liked what they saw. During Pittsburgh's run to the Cup, naysayers doubted Fleury's abilities and many said that Pittsburgh didn't have a hope because Fleury notoriously made a costly error at some point during each game. But he proved them all wrong, especially in the final minutes, even seconds, of the seventh game where his two unbelievable saves helped secure his team the opportunity to hoist the Stanley Cup in victory. The first shot came from the point. Fleury made the save, though gave up a rebound that landed right on the stick of Detroit's, Nicklas Lidstrom who quickly fired the puck and sent Fleury diving cross net to stop it. He made both saves within seconds and secured a 2-1 victory for his team.

This was Pittsburgh's, and Fleury's, second straight year in the Stanley Cup finals. They didn't win in 2008, but they put forth a good showing against the experienced and skillful Detroit Red Wings and Fleury was instrumental in getting them there.

Image provided by Hockey Canada

Marc-André Fleury won the hearts of fans in Halifax at the 2003 IIHF World Junior Championship. Canada lost to Russia in the final game, but the IIHF still awarded Fleury the tournament's top goaltender award.

Pittsburgh Penguins

Hockey heroes:
**Martin Brodeur,
Patrick Roy**

Favourite TV show:
Prison Break

Activities outside of hockey:
fishing, water sports

If not a hockey player
would be a:
police officer

Best concert ever attended:
Britney Spears

Favourite band:
Nickelback

Most memorable minor
hockey experience:
**winning Quebec Peewee
tournament**

Favourite magazine:
**Men's Health, Dupont
Registry**

Person who had most influence
on hockey career growing up:
father

August 2009 orientation camp

Marc-André Fleury

Fleury is a true butterfly goalie and has great flexibility. He also plays the puck well, and has solid lateral movement—meaning he can quickly get from post to post to stop the puck.

Fleury has made some significant contributions to Hockey Canada. Beginning in 2001 and playing for the Canadian Under-18 Men's Summer Team he earned a gold medal at the Six Nations Cup in the Czech Republic. From there, he followed the natural progression to the World Junior Team, winning silver medals in 2003 and 2004. In 2003 the World Junior Championship was played in Halifax, Nova Scotia, and although Canada lost in the gold medal game to Russia, Fleury was named the tournament's top goaltender. Rarely does the goalie from the losing team take the top honours, but Fleury played so well that the IIHF awarded him the honours. This was Fleury's first glance at the limelight as his show-stopping saves during that tournament made him a hero in Halifax. The fans loved to chant his name over and over during every game. This adoration only fueled his game, and he became better under the hype.

This great performance at the World Juniors saw Fleury ranked number one going into the 2003 NHL Entry Draft where Pittsburgh picked him first overall. Being drafted number one is exciting, but comes with intense pressure and expectations. Fleury appeared in his first NHL game on October 10, 2003, and made an incredible 46 saves, (one defending a penalty shot) in a game that the Penguins lost 3-0. Early in his first season, Fleury

2009 August orientation camp

exceeded expectations and earned rookie-of-the-month honours in October. But his luck soon ended and following the 2004 IIHF World Junior Championship, where Canada had given up a 3-1 lead going into the third to lose 4-3, Fleury returned home to learn that he was being sent back to the Quebec Major Junior Hockey League (QMJHL). One of the goals at the World Juniors occurred when Fleury came out of his net to clear the puck but it hit defenceman Braydon Coburn and bounced into the net.

Instead of jumping back into the NHL the following season, he was assigned to Pittsburgh's American Hockey League affiliate, which actually worked well for Fleury because the NHL was on lockout anyway.

The season after the labour disputes ended, Fleury was still assigned to the minors. Not long into the season, he was called up to play with Pittsburgh, and he made the best of it. He played well, but he did not maintain a starting role. Fleury played the duration of the season between the NHL and the AHL. His career seemed to be one of ups and downs, though finally in 2006 his play secured him an active spot with the Penguins and, well, the rest is history.

Now he is being considered for the 2010 Canadian Olympic Team, which is an amazing accomplishment, since he was in the minors just a little more than four years ago. Marc-André Fleury's dynamic play has given his name great weight and his skills and big game experience make him a definite contender for Team Canada. He has definitely played his way into the young up-and-coming goalie group.

Camp Update

All the young goalies played well in the intersquad game. Fleury played on Team White and split the game with Brodeur playing 30 minutes total. He had ten shots on net and made nine saves. He was also in net for the shootout at the end, letting in goals by Marleau, Heatley, Morrow, Carter and Doan. Although he didn't put on the show that Brodeur and Luongo did, he was solid and effective.

Statistics– International											
Year	Team	Event	GP	MIN	GA	SO	GAA	W-L-T	SOG	SV%	Result
Regional											
2001	QUE	WU17	2	119	6	0	3.03	0-1-1	82	0.927	9th
National											
2001	CAN	SU18	1	60	3	0	2.00	0-1-0	20	0.850	Gold
2003	CAN	WJC	5	267	7	1	1.57	3-1-0	97	0.928	Silver
2004	CAN	WJC	5	298	9	1	1.81	3-1-0	108	0.917	Silver
	CAN	INTL TOTAL	11	625	19	2	1.82	6-3-0	225	0.916	
	CAN	SR TOTAL	-	-	-	-	-	-	-	-	

ROBERTO LUONGO

GOALTENDER #1

Catches: **Left**
Height: **6'3"**
Weight: **205 lbs**
Birthdate: **April 4, 1979**
Birthplace: **Montreal, QC**
Hometown: **Montreal, QC**
Team: **Vancouver Canucks (NHL)**
MHA: **AHM St. Léonard**
NHL Draft: **New York Islanders: 1997 (1, 4)**
Last Amateur Club: **Acadie-Bathurst Titan (QMJHL)**

Since the 2004 World Cup, Roberto Luongo has been Team Canada's "heir apparent." He has been the designated guy and he rightfully, because of his skill and commitment to Hockey Canada, has taken his place on the bench playing behind Martin Brodeur. Like a good prince he has waited patiently and has been there when called upon to play for his country. At the 2004 World Cup, Luongo replaced an injured Brodeur to start the semifinal game. He played incredibly and made 37 out of 40 saves to beat the Czech's in a 4-3 overtime game. Yes, he came up with a big one. He knows his role, plays it well, but has matured over the years and soon it will be his time to overthrow the king. The big question is: will he make his big move at the 2010 Olympics?

The captain of the Vancouver Canucks sealed his spot on this orientation-camp roster last year, even though his NHL team suffered a devastating loss to the Chicago Blackhawks in round two of the 2009 NHL playoffs. Visibly upset after Vancouver was defeated in the sixth game of the series (Chicago took the series four games to two), an emotional Luongo appeared on television to announce that he felt responsible for the loss and that he had let his team down. Luongo is just one of those goalies who shoulders the blame. He felt that by letting in the shots that he had, (seven goals), that he had ruined the entire season for his team. At that moment, reeling from the loss, Luongo had forgotten that he had stood on his head at the end of the season to help his team win the Northwest Division title.

The Hockey Canada management staff knew that Luongo still had many good games in him—the type of games that make

Roberto Luongo grew up in Montreal, QC. He played most of his minor hockey career in St. Léonard. His parents always encouraged him to play out instead of as a goalie, but he had a mind of his own.

Vancouver Canucks

August 2009 orientation camp

Hockey Hero:
Grant Fuhr

Favourite movie:
Shawshank Redemption

If not a hockey player
would be a:
poker player

Best concert ever attended:
Nickelback

Favourite band:
U2

Most memorable minor
hockey experience:
**winning Peewee AA
tournament in Repentigny**

Favourite magazine:
Fluff

Favourite book:
**Daniel Negreanau:
Small Ball Approach**

Roberto Luongo

Luongo making a key save in the semifinal game at the 2004 World Cup of Hockey in Toronto. Canada beat the Czechs 4-3 in overtime.

television announcers go ballistic because he can move to make those spectacular saves that leave the crowd in awe. The coaching staff knew that because of his character, he wouldn't let that bad game haunt him, but instead it would make him hungry to win. Even after that loss, Steve Yzerman and the rest of the crew still had Luongo at the top of the list for many reasons, the biggest being his presence. He is a dominant goalie mentally and physically.

In his teens, Luongo played in the QMJHL for the Val-d'Or Foreurs and in his first season only had six wins in 23 games. The next year, as a starting goaltender, he bumped his stats up a notch by winning 32 games and taking home the Mike Bossy Trophy as the league's best professional prospect. His name became a buzz word with scouts, and when it came time for the 1997 NHL Entry Draft, Luongo went first round, fourth overall to the New York Islanders to become, at that time, the highest picked goaltender in NHL history. But he didn't make the jump to the NHL immediately and instead continued his junior career. Sparks flew for Luongo in his next season (1997-98), especially when he took his team to the Memorial Cup finals.

His NHL debut was on November 28, 1999, and wearing a New York Islanders jersey he stopped 43 shots for a 2-1 win against the Boston Bruins.

The next spring, Luongo was traded to the Florida Panthers and he worked hard and long to become the Panthers starting goaltender. Steadily, he rose to the top and in the 2003-04 season, he earned his first Vezina Trophy nomination as the league's most valuable goaltender, becoming the runner-up to Martin Brodeur. This honour would happen one more time for Luongo in 2007 but by then the Florida Panthers had traded him. Just before the 2006-07 season, Luongo was sent packing to a new home with a view of a different ocean and started in goal with the Vancouver Canucks. That spring he was nominated for the Vezina Trophy and once again, he was runner-up to Martin Brodeur. Life in Vancouver has been good for Luongo but he has been plagued with injuries in the last two years of his career.

Luongo has everything he needs to be successful and be named as one of the goalies for this Olympic Team. His biggest challenge is his history of injuries. If he stays healthy, and plays well all fall, chances for Luongo making it this time are good. Will he overthrow the king? Stay tuned.

Camp Highlights
In the first period Luongo was the Team Red's goalie, and Brodeur was in net for Team White. Luongo lived up to Brodeur's challenge and was amazing enough to earn chants of Loooooo from the crowd. He was peppered with 17 shots and made 17 saves. Both veteran goalies put on a show and when the first period was over the score was 0-0. In the Calgary Herald, Luongo was given the second star of the Red and White Scrimmage.

		Statistics– **International**									
Year	Team	Event	GP	MIN	GA	SO	GAA	W-L-T	SOG	SV%	Result
					Regional						
1995	QC	WU17	4	224	13	n/a	3.49	n/a	79	0.848	Bronze
					National						
1998	CAN	WJC	3	146	9	0	3.70	0-2-0	71	0.901	8th
1999	CAN	WJC	7	405	12	2	1.92	4-2-1	224	0.942	Silver
2001	CAN	WHC	2	83	2	0	1.44	2-0-0	39	0.949	5th
2003	CAN	WHC	4	212	7	1	1.98	4-0-0	100	0.930	Gold
2004	CAN	WHC	7	440	17	1	2.32	5-1-1	211	0.919	Gold
2004	CAN	WC	1	64	3	0	2.82	1-0-0	40	0.925	Gold
2005	CAN	WHC	2	120	3	1	1.50	1-0-1	43	0.930	Silver
2006	CAN	OLY	2	119	3	0	1.51	1-0-1	42	0.929	7th
	CAN	INTL TOTAL	28	1589	57	5	2.15	18-5-4	770	0.926	
	CAN	SR TOTAL	18	1038	36	3	2.08	14-1-3	475	0.924	

Roberto Luongo

STEVE MASON

GOALTENDER #1

Catches: **Right**
Height: **6'4"**
Weight: **212 lbs**
Birthdate: **May 9, 1988**
Birthplace: **Oakville, Ont.**
Hometown: **Oakville, Ont.**
Team: **Columbus Blue Jackets (NHL)**
MHA: **Oakville MHA**
NHL Draft: **Columbus Blue Jackets: 2006 (3, 69)**
Last Amateur Club: **Kitchener Rangers (OHL)**

The Hockey Canada management team describes 21-year-old Steve Mason as young but an all-star junior who's ready to make the natural progression into the world of international men's hockey. Yes, this is his first sojourn into international competition that is not classified as Junior but the management team thinks he is ready. Goalies normally take many years to develop and find the confidence and skill needed for Olympic play, but this young netminder has shown such talent already that he earned an invitation to orientation camp.

So, how does a kid this young get invited to a camp for such a prestigious team as Canada's Olympic squad? How do such great hockey legends sit in a room and discuss goalie after goalie yet put such a young kid on the orientation-camp roster? There are a lot of great NHL goalies who didn't make the grade. The management team invited him because they knew this young player was an exceptionally skilled and focused player and they didn't want a repeat of the Crosby incident in 2006. Age was not going to be a factor. Crosby wasn't invited to the orientation camp in 2006 because he was said to be too young and in post discussions Hockey Canada realized that age shouldn't determine whether or not a player is invited to camp. Instead, they looked at skill, focus, accountability, and trustworthiness.

Mason had a great season in 2008-09 with the Columbus Blue Jackets. Simple as that, his stats tell his story. And stats do count when picking these teams. Those papers are always on the table when players are being picked. For the first time ever, the Columbus Blue Jackets made the playoffs and they feel that this

In 2007, Steve Mason won the OHL Goaltender of the Year award at an awards banquet at the Hockey Hall of Fame.

2009 August orientation camp

Columbus Blue Jackets

Favourite movie:
Friday Night Lights

Favourite TV show:
The Office

Favourite activities outside of hockey:
golf, movies

If not a hockey player would be a:
firefighter, pilot

Person who had most influence
on career growing up:
Dave Rook (coach), parents

Favourite band:
Nickelback

Hockey hero:
Martin Brodeur

Favourite book:
**The Hatchet,
by Gary Paulsen**

Steve Mason

CANADA

success had something to do with the rookie who was minding the net. The young lad notched 10 shutouts in one season of play, the first time this feat has been accomplished by a rookie in 15 years. Tony Esposito had 15 as a rookie in 1969-70.

Mason is a big boy, and a technically sound goalie. Rick Nash has been quoted as saying that Mason, "reminds him of Roberto Luongo the way he closes off the whole bottom part of the net and is still big and quick enough to stop the high shots."

His positional play is great and that is proof of his ability to think the game through. He is young, but self-assured and plays with a mature poise. Ken Hitchcock loves him, and knows he has that competitive edge and focus needed to stay in the big games. Mason knows how to make key saves. From his training with goalie coaches along the way, Mason plays aggressively but knows how to have patience, especially when he goes from post to post.

This young goalie didn't strap on the pads when he was just a little guy like a lot of other goalies do. He played forward until he was ten, then with money he had saved from having a paper route, he bought some goalie pads. He may have started a little later but he has made up the time by honing his skills.

Mason's rap sheet for awards might not be as long as some of the other players trying out for the team and he certainly wasn't the player who went first overall in the NHL Entry Draft, (he went third round sixty-ninth overall in 2006) but he is still a goalie to watch. And he does have some Hockey Canada experience. In 2008, he won a gold medal when he played on the IIHF World Junior Team in the Czech Republic, being named top goaltender and most valuable player at that tournament. He also helped Canada capture the Canada/Russia Super Series in August/September 2007 by recording two wins.

Can he make Team Canada? Only time will tell. He is competing against his hockey hero, Martin Brodeur. In fact, at his home in Oakville, a poster of Martin Brodeur still hangs on his bedroom wall. Now here he is, early in his twenties and strapping on his pads to try to take the in-demand spot away from his hero.

It is exciting to see such young talent continue to develop in Canada's Junior Hockey programs. For our nation to rank among the top in the world, it is important that enrollment in hockey remain strong and that today's youth play with determination and spirit so that when the stars of today retire, a new breed of heroes emerge to represent our nation. Mason is young, though possesses much of what a team leading goaltender requires to make it to the Olympic level. Will he make those key saves for Canada that Ken Hitchcock knows that he can?

2009 August orientation camp

Camp Highlights

Mason played a good game in net, as did all the young goalies, proving that the depth in the Canadian goaltenders runs mighty deep. He played on Team White with Luongo and Ward and they each played a period. Mason had 13 shots and made 13 saves. As Mason was in net for the third period, he also played in the shootout, giving up three goals to Crosby, St. Louis and Eric Staal. Steve Mason was also eager to ask Martin Brodeur for an autograph.

							Statistics– **International**				
Year	Team	Event	GP	MIN	GA	SO	GAA	W-L-T	SOG	SV%	Result
						Regional					
						Not applicable					
						National					
2007	CAN	SS	3	150	6	0	2.40	2-0-0	92	0.938	1st
2008	CAN	WJC	5	304	6	1	1.19	5-0-0	123	0.951	Gold
	CAN	INTL TOTAL	8	454	12	1	1.59	7-0-0	215	0.944	
	CAN	SR TOTAL	-	-	-	-	-	-	-	-	

Steve Mason

CAM WARD

GOALTENDER #30

Catches : **Left**
Height: **6'1"**
Weight: **200 lbs**
Birthdate: **February 29, 1984**
Birthplace: **Saskatoon, Sask.**
Hometown: **Sherwood Park, Alta.**
Team: **Carolina Hurricanes (NHL)**
MHA: **Sherwood Park MHA**
NHL Draft: **Carolina Hurricanes: 2002 (1, 25)**
Last Amateur Club: **Red Deer Rebels (WHL)**

L ike Mason and Fleury, Cam Ward is a member of the exclusive up-and-coming young goalie club that has some Hockey Canada experience, great skill, poise and energy. Ward also grew up emulating Martin Brodeur like the other two young goalies. Interesting how all these young goalies list Marty as their hero and now here they are competing against him for a spot on Team Canada's 2010 Olympic roster.

The young ones are ready but is a vet like Brodeur willing to give up his coveted spot? He does still rein as the king but there are a lot of young men-in-waiting.

Even though Ward watched Brodeur on television when he was a kid and worked hard to play like him, he is now a goalie who definitely plays the classic butterfly style. Along with his honed style, he has many other fine skills. He positions himself in front of the opposing shooter and cuts down the angles well, has terrific lateral movement, is lightening fast with his glove hand, and has an uncanny knack of seeing through screens. He also doesn't give up many rebounds and stands technically solid in his net. Plus, he is known to confidently use the paddle-down technique where he gets his stick right down on the ice to stop those nasty little wrap-arounds and scrambles where players are just trying to slide the puck along the ice and into the net. Those who have had the pleasure of working with Cam Ward say he has a great attitude.

The Hockey Canada management team made notes on this young goalie. One thing they wrote down was that he was not fazed by the limelight. This is a good thing. A goalie is often put under the spotlight and the media can be downright nasty, especially

Image provided by his mother, Laurel Ward

Cam Ward played his minor hockey career in Sherwood Park. Here, he is with the Sherwood Park Royals Peewee A.

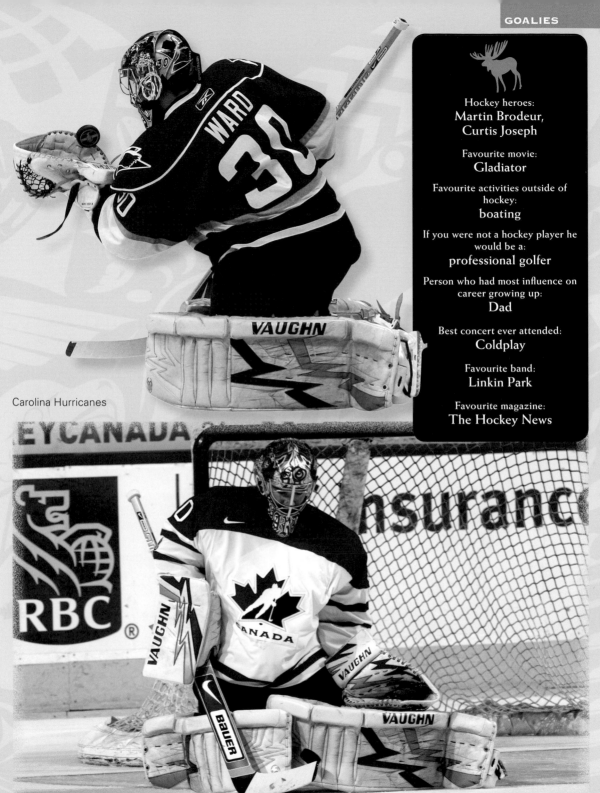

Carolina Hurricanes

Hockey heroes:
**Martin Brodeur,
Curtis Joseph**

Favourite movie:
Gladiator

Favourite activities outside of hockey:
boating

If you were not a hockey player he would be a:
professional golfer

Person who had most influence on career growing up:
Dad

Best concert ever attended:
Coldplay

Favourite band:
Linkin Park

Favourite magazine:
The Hockey News

2009 August orientation camp

Cam Ward

when it comes to Team Canada playing at home for an Olympic medal. A few soft goals could make for some cruel attention.

This young player knows the ups and downs of professional sport. In 2002, at the ripe age of 18, Cam Ward was cut from Canada's National Junior Team. Making the World Junior Team had been a goal that he had set for himself when he was a youngster. Horribly upset, Ward continued his year with the Red Deer Rebels, trying to put his disappointment behind him.

It's a good thing he didn't let his disappointment get the best of him as at the 2002 NHL Entry Draft, Ward went twenty-fifth in the first round to the Carolina Hurricanes. Though instead of making an immediate jump to the NHL, he continued playing with the Rebels; leading them twice to the WHL finals. Ward then played two years in the AHL for the Lowell Lock Monsters after he finished his Junior career. On a note of interest, Ward was also cut from the Canadian World Junior team in 2003.

It took until 2004 before Carolina showed some interest in Ward, and gave him a contract to sign. But that didn't mean they were going to use him right away and they didn't until his debut game on October 5, 2005. It was Carolina's season opener and Ward was called upon because the Hurricane's number one goalie, Martin Gerber, got injured during the course of the game. Ward came off the bench and showed his stuff, stopping 10 out of 11 shots during his time in the game. Ward's next game caught the attention of fans and the media alike. Two days after his NHL debut, with Gerber still injured, Ward took to the net in a game against the Pittsburgh Penguins. The game went to a tie and then a shootout. In the

one-on-one battle between goalie and player, Ward stopped Mario Lemieux and Sidney Crosby to help the Hurricanes win 3-2.

In 2006, Ward was a key player in the Hurricanes' jaunt to the Cup. At first it didn't appear that Ward would get much ice time but then Gerber struggled and the Hurricanes gave Cam the starting position. With Ward in net, the Hurricanes beat Montreal then went on to beat the New Jersey Devils and Martin Brodeur—Ward's hero. The Hurricanes continued on the road to the Cup and ended up in the finals pitted against the Edmonton Oilers where Ward became the first rookie goalie in 20 years to earn a shutout in the Stanley Cup Finals. After the game good things were still to come for Ward as he earned the right to be the first rookie goaltender to win the Conn Smythe Trophy since 1987.

Canada has an incredible pool of talent from which to build its national teams. Ward may have not played for Canada's World Junior Team but he has successfully played for Canada at the Men's World Championships in both 2007 and 2008. In 2007, in Moscow, Ward was given the nod to play in the semifinal game and rose to the challenge. His stellar play secured him the spot of starting goalie for the final game and when he helped Canada secure the gold medal win, the Hockey Canada management team were definitely impressed.

The scrutiny that each candidate faces is intense and the expectations of a nation and team management are fierce. Timing is everything. Ward may not have secured a spot on a Canadian World Junior Team, but all of that is history. He has continued to improve and earned his right to be invited to the orientation camp for the 2010 Olympic Team Canada.

Camp Highlights
Ward was told to sit out the first ice session because of an injury and this was definitely not what he wanted to hear. He kept asking when he could play. He did hit the ice for the second ice time and he played solid in net. As with all the young goalies, Ward played well the night of the Red and White game. He played the second period for the White team, stopping 10 out of 12 shots.

Statistics– International											
Year	Team	Event	GP	MIN	GA	SO	GAA	W-L-T	SOG	SV%	Result
Regional											
Not applicable											
National											
2007	CAN	WHC	5	300	11	0	2.20	5-0-0	130	0.915	Gold
2008	CAN	WHC	5	303	13	0	2.58	4-1-0	130	0.900	Silver
	CAN	INTL TOTAL	10	603	24	0	2.39	9-1-0	260	0.908	
	CAN	SR TOTAL	10	603	24	0	2.39	9-1-0	260	0.908	

FRANCOIS BEAUCHEMIN

DEFENCE #23

Shoots: **Left**
Height: **6'0"**
Weight: **213 lbs**
Birthdate: **June 4, 1980**
Birthplace: **Sorel, QC**
Hometown: **Sorel, QC**
Team: **Toronto Maple Leafs (NHL)**
MHA: **AHM Sorel**
NHL Draft: **Montreal Canadiens: 1998 (3, 75)**
Last Amateur Club: **Moncton Wildcats (QMJHL)**

CANADA

There is only one player selected to this roster who has never played on a Hockey Canada team and Quebec-born Francois Beauchemin is the guy. Obviously, this player was not invited to the orientation camp for his international experience as he has none. It's not often that a player without international experience can crack a HC roster. How did he get this far in his career without some HC stats beside his name?

According to the Hockey Canada management team, Beauchemin is just someone they couldn't leave off the invitation list. We all know that players like Beauchemin can make their way to the top. He moves the puck well, he has deceiving offence and he has seen success in the playoffs. He played a big defensive roll for the Anaheim Ducks in 2007 when they won the Stanley Cup.

Beauchemin played his Junior career in the QMJHL, and he was certainly a good player, but not good enough to be invited to tryout for Canada's World Junior Team.

Then in 1998 he was drafted by the Montreal Canadiens, seventy-fifth overall but he immediately returned to the QMJHL for two more seasons; helping his team win the President's Cup as league champions in 1999. When he turned pro in 2000-01 he didn't initially enter the NHL, but instead played for four additional years in the minors.

During the lockout year in 2004-05, instead of making the trek overseas like many players did, he stayed in the AHL for the season. Francois Beauchemin has been known to say that, he thinks his biggest life lesson was taught over the five years he played in the AHL, working harder every year to make it to the NHL.

Francois Beauchemin played for the QMJHL Acadie-Bathurst Titan team for two years.

Image provided by Gilles Corteau of the QMJHL

Favourite activities
outside of hockey:
fishing

If not a hockey player
would be a:
farmer

Hockey hero:
Raymond Bourque

Person who had most influence on
hockey career growing up:
Andre Gavel (coach)

Best concert ever attended:
AC/DC

Pre-game meal:
chicken and pasta

Favourite team growing up:
Montreal Canadiens

2009 August orientation camp

Francois Beauchemin

There is something to be said about persistence. His NHL debut happened in the fall of 2005 and he put in 11 games with the Columbus Blue Jackets before he was traded to the Anaheim Ducks.

Following the trade, he settled in, found his game and quickly became considered one of the top-four defencemen on the Anaheim Ducks. His previous hard work, and persistence to make it one day, was starting to pay off and earning a key pivotal defence role and the support of the Anaheim franchise gave him the confidence to help his team win the 2007 Stanley Cup.

Toronto Maple Leafs

And this is when he started to gain the recognition of the Hockey Canada team. What exactly was said about Francois Beauchemin behind closed doors that gave him the green light to attend the August camp?

He's not one of Canada's up-and-coming young ones but certainly not one of the old guard either. Born in 1980, he will be 30 at the Olympic Games.

The word in the boardroom is that he makes a great first pass. This management staff is definitely looking at players who can move the puck up the ice and out of the defensive zone. In international hockey, the defence need to move the puck quickly so the forwards can move up the ice and toward the opposing team's net. The Russians have some big players that can do some serious damage if the puck is not moved fast enough. The passes have to be long and strong and accurate. They have to go tape to tape and they have to be solid enough so the receiver doesn't break stride. Beauchemin has that very specific skill and he is darn good at it.

CANADA

It also helps that he is a good size. He is not huge, (6 feet tall and 218 lbs) but he does put every inch of his body to good use on the ice by playing a physical game. He is definitely a defenceman to be reckoned with. Just recently, in early July, Beauchemin signed a three-year-contract with the Toronto Maple Leafs. Toronto GM, Brian Burke told the media, "Francois will be a welcome addition to our blue line. He's a rock solid, steady defender that will add character to our team."

Beauchemin may be a late bloomer, and an inexperienced international player, but he has proven that he possesses good skills, which was enough to invite him to the August camp. Don't ever underestimate the power of the underdog, especially one as persistent as Beauchemin.

Camp Highlights
The word is out that that Beauchemin had a good orientation camp and a great scrimmage. He was paired with Eric Staal and played his game, moving the puck well out of the zone, and playing his "rock solid" style of game.

2009 August orientation camp

		Statistics– International						
Year	Team	Event	GP	G	A	PTS	PIM	Result
		Regional						
		Not applicable						
		National						
		Not applicable						
	CAN	INTL TOTAL	0	0	0	0	0	

Francois Beauchemin

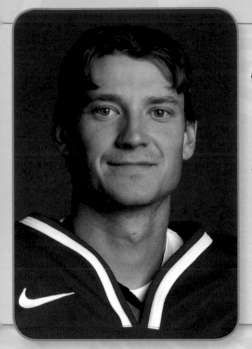

JAY BOUWMEESTER

DEFENCE #4

Shoots: **Left**
Height: **6'4"**
Weight: **218 lbs**
Birthdate: **September 27, 1983**
Birthplace: **Edmonton, Alta.**
Hometown: **Edmonton, Alta.**
Team: **Calgary Flames (NHL)**
MHA: **Millwoods MHA**
NHL Draft: **Florida Panthers: 2002 (1, 3)**
Last Amateur Club: **Medicine Hat Tigers (WHL)**

CANADA

This quiet, unassuming giant has tons of international experience. Bouwmeester started playing for Team Canada in 2000 when he was still in his teens. He turned 16 on September 27, and that Christmas, he boarded a plane for Sweden where he took to the ice wearing the red and white Canadian jersey. Every young, talented hockey player yearns to play on the Canadian World Junior team and many, many good twenty year olds get left at home.

So how did such a young kid make it?

It helped that at the ripe age of 16, Bouwmeester was 6'4" and 195 pounds—giving him a size advantage that the game of hockey loves so much. He was a strong force on the blue line, simple as that. Bouwmeester started collecting his Hockey Canada medals early. That year, the Canadian Junior team won the bronze medal by defeating the USA in a game that ended in a shootout. Bouwmeester returned to Canada that January with a coveted medal and went back to his Grade 11 classmates at the Medicine Hat high school he was attending because he was already playing in the WHL for the Medicine Hat Tigers. He still holds the record as youngest ever to be on the National Junior team.

After that first year, Bouwmeester went on to make the World Junior team two more times. In 2001 he picked up another bronze medal and in 2002 he came home with a silver medal. He is one of only six players to play for Canada's World Junior team at three IIHF World Junior Championships.

Bouwmeester's experience doesn't end with the Canadian World Junior team, and he has picked up a few more medals along

Image provided by Hockey Canada (2001)

Jay Bouwmeester at 17, in his second year playing for the IIHF World Junior Team.

2009 August orientation camp

Jay Bouwmeester

First minor hockey team:
Millwood Bruins

Minor hockey association:
Millwoods MHA

If not a hockey player would be a:
construction worker

Favourite food:
steak

Favourite movie:
Dumb and Dumber

Hockey Hero:
Steve Yzerman

Favourite activities
outside of hockey:
golf, mountain bike

the way. He has played on three World Championship teams (2003, 2004, 2008), on the World Cup team (2004), and he was a late roster addition to the 2006 Olympic team when Scott Niedermayer had to bow out because of injuries. He picked up gold medals in the World Championships in 2003 and 2004.

But is experience enough to earn Jay Bouwmeester a final spot on the 2010 roster?

The management team looks at more than experience and Bouwmeester has many other attributes. For a big guy, he has great mobility on the ice. North to south, east to west, he can move. He also sees both sides of the ice, which is something that the management team is really looking for. They want versatile two-way defencemen.

What the Hockey Canada staff love about Bouwmeester is his ability to chew up heavy playing minutes. He is a player that can average 30-plus minutes of ice time per game without difficulty. Dependable on the bench, he is the guy the coaches can call on for first unit power play and first unit penalty kill. Size and strength give him that edge to get out there and get the job done in every situation. He can play the shut-down role or he can blend in with the solid core. Bottom line, he is a guy who can be called on during crunch time.

Over the years, Bouwmeester has seen his share of ups and downs and much has been written about him being overrated, not producing and not being the force that the hockey world thinks he should be. He was so good so young then he tapered off a bit, or maybe just leveled out for a few years. But in 2008, Bouwmeester kicked his game up a notch. There was a noticeable improvement and he seemed to suddenly mature again. Not in size this time, but

Calgary Flames

in his mental game. This leap definitely helped him get an invite to the August orientation camp.

Jay Bouwmeester was traded from the Florida Panthers to the Calgary Flames in June of 2009. This fresh start might give him the jolt he needs to be a force that the Canadian team so needs and wants from this young man.

According to the Hockey Canada management team, Bouwmeester is the kind of player who "does nothing great but does everything well."

Camp Highlights

Bouwmeester was paired with Brent Burns. The non-contact approach, that was the philosophy of the camp, made it hard for some defencemen, like Bouwmeester, to really show their game. As with all players, he will get a good look in the fall. In the Red and White game, Jay did receive a healthy roar from the Calgary crowd when he tripped up Jason Spezza in the second period and had to head to the box for an interference penalty.

2009 August orientation camp

Statistics— **International**								
Year	Team	Event	GP	G	A	PTS	PIM	Result
		Regional						
1999	AB	CWG		unavailable				Gold
		National						
2000	CAN	WJC	7	0	0	0	2	Bronze
2001	CAN	WJC	7	0	2	2	6	Bronze
2002	CAN	WJC	7	0	2	2	10	Silver
2003	CAN	WHC	9	3	4	7	4	Gold
2004	CAN	WHC	9	2	1	3	0	Gold
2004	CAN	WC	4	0	0	0	0	1st
2006	CAN	OLY	6	0	0	0	0	7th
2008	CAN	WHC	9	0	0	0	4	Silver
	CAN	INTL TOTAL	58	5	9	14	26	
	CAN	SR TOTAL	37	5	5	10	8	

Jay Bouwmeester

DAN BOYLE

DEFENCE #22

Shoots: **Right**
Height: **5'11"**
Weight: **190 lbs**
Birthdate: **July 12, 1976**
Birthplace: **Ottawa, Ont.**
Hometown: **Ottawa, Ont.**
Team: **San Jose Sharks (NHL)**
MHA: **Ottawa West MHA**
NHL Draft: **Undrafted**
Last Amateur Club: **University of Miami (Ohio) (CCHA)**

CANADA

Gutsy, strong, and a true competitor, Dan Boyle earned the right to be an invitee for the August camp. He plays physical and isn't afraid of anyone, even though he is only 5'11"—small for a blue-line player. He skates well and has that great mobility that the Hockey Canada management team is looking for. They want quickness in the back end—players who can turn on a dime and move the puck out of the zone.

One thing that Dan Boyle lacks is a great deal of Hockey Canada experience. He has only represented Hockey Canada twice, once in 2006 at the Olympics as an alternate player, and when he played on the Men's World Team at the 2005 IIHF World Championship in Austria. He came home with a silver medal that year, his only medal with Team Canada. That's the entirety of his international experience. But the Hockey Canada management team will say that not having Boyle play in the 2006 Olympics in Turin, "was a big mistake."

Boyle's route to the NHL has also been a little different than a lot of the players selected for the 2010 roster. He is one of a few who skipped the Major Junior route and went to the National Collegiate Athletic Association (NCAA) instead. After four years at Miami University in Ohio, Boyle then made the jump to the NHL and was signed as a free agent by the Florida Panthers. Okay, so he is also one of the few players at the orientation camp who was never drafted by the NHL. After signing as a free agent, he played his first few seasons with the Panther's farm team in the American Hockey League. Proving himself a competitor in the AHL, Boyle

Dan Boyle grew up in Ottawa, playing summer hockey with Ottawa 67's team.

Image provided by Tom Roly of the San Jose Sharks

Hockey Heros:
Rick Tocchet, Brian Leetch

Favourite TV show:
Conan O'Brien

If not a hockey player would be a:
singer in a band

Person who had most influence
on hockey career growing up:
parents

Favourite band:
Faith No More

Most memorable
hockey experience:
first hat trick

Favourite team growing up:
Philadelphia Flyers

Favourite magazine:
Maxim

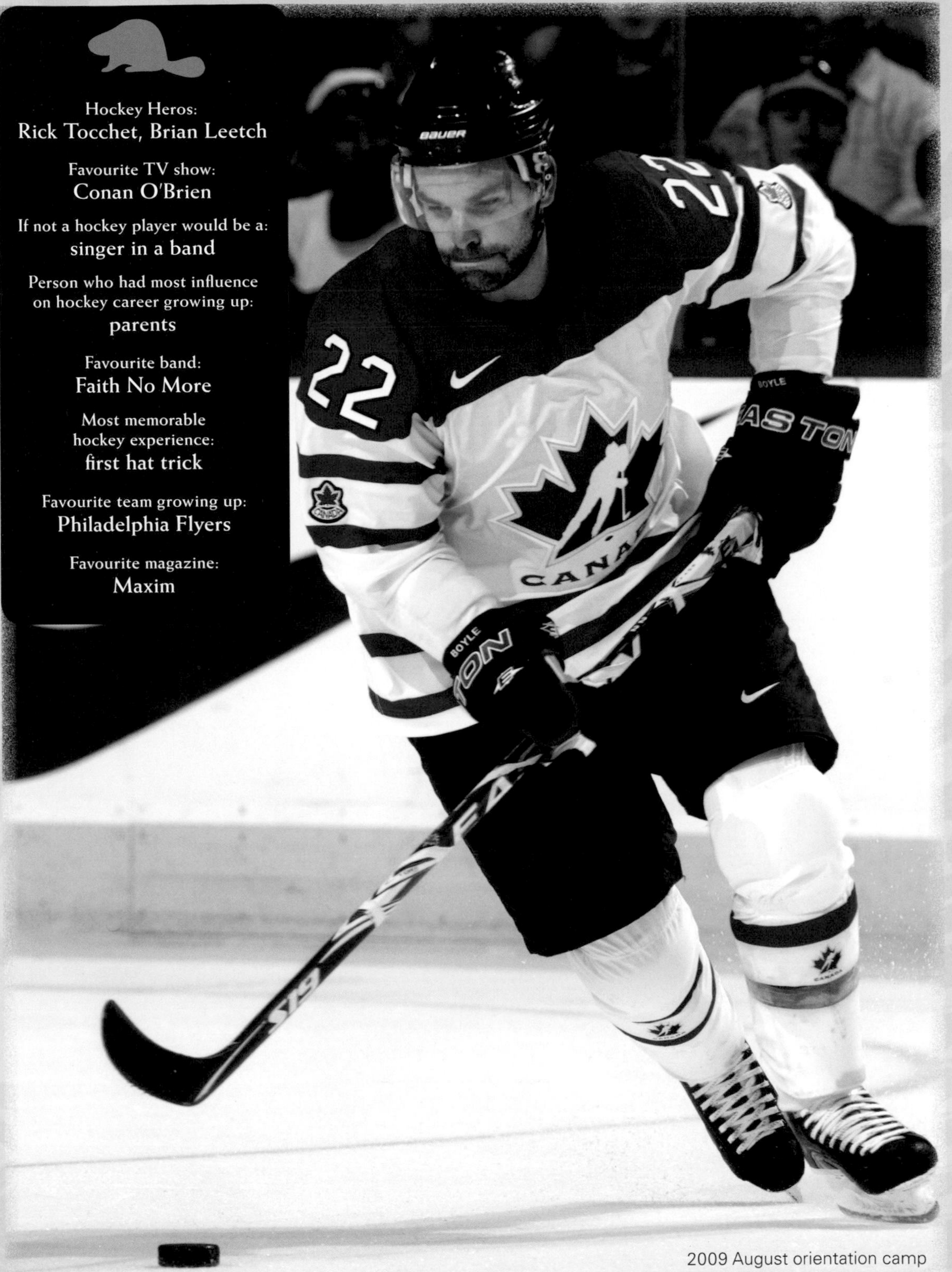

2009 August orientation camp

Dan Boyle

cracked the full-time NHL roster in Florida in 2000 and played there until he was traded to Tampa the next year.

So why is the Hockey Canada management team saying they made a mistake in not having Boyle in 2006? There are lots of good skaters and competitors in the NHL.

The answer is obvious: Dan Boyle is a defenceman who is a gifted offensive player. The time which he has spent with the Tampa Bay Lightning established this for him. He played six years with Tampa before he was traded to the San Jose Sharks in 2008. In sunny Tampa, he played behind stars such as Vincent Lecavalier, Martin St. Louis and Brad Richards and in his first season, posted 13 goals and 40 assists for a 53 point season. Then in 2004, he definitely helped his team win the Stanley Cup Championship even though he only managed to record 39 points for the season. He may not have as much international experience as some of the other players, but he does have championship experience and a Stanley Cup ring goes a long way with the Hockey Canada management team. It proves he can play in the pressure-cooker games.

San Jose Sharks

As a defenceman, Dan Boyle earned his first hat trick with the Tampa Bay Lightning on December 23, 2006 playing against the New York Rangers. Boyle added an assist that night for a four-point game. That same season, Boyle took his scoring to an all-time high when he recorded 20 goals and 43 assists for a 63 point season. He set the franchise record for goals by a defenceman and he also earned fourth spot in scoring for Tampa.

In 2007 Boyle suffered a freak accident when a skate blade fell from a shelf and landed on his arm, severing

Canada vs. Russia at the 2005 IIHF Men's World Championship in Vienna and Innsbruck. Canada placed second overall to the Czechs.

some tendons. He only played 37 games that season and by spring the rumours were flying that he would be traded. Before long, he was.

For the 2008-09 season, Boyle played for the San Jose Sharks. With San Jose he continued his scoring and logged 14 goals and 35 assists, for a total of 49 points.

Despite his size, it is these offensive skills coupled with the fact that he is a physical competitor that has earned him the right to be at the August orientation camp.

Camp Highlights
Boyle was matched up with Pronger at the Red and White game and they proved they were an extremely strong tandem by complimenting each other's strengths. Playing on the right side, Boyle moved the puck efficiently and quickly.

Statistics– **International**							
Year	Team	Event	GP	G	A	PTS	PIM	Result
Regional							
Not applicable							
National							
2005	CAN	WHC	9	0	3	3	6	Silver
2006	CAN	OLY	--	--	--	--	--	7th
	CAN	INTL TOTAL	9	0	3	3	6	

Dan Boyle

BRENT BURNS

DEFENCE #8

Shoots: **Right**
Height: **6'5"**
Weight: **219 lbs**
Birthdate: **March 9, 1985**
Birthplace: **Ajax, Ont.**
Hometown: **Barrie, Ont.**
Team: **Minnesota Wild (NHL)**
MHA: **Greater Toronto Hockey League (GTHL)**
NHL Draft: **Minnesota Wild: 2003 (1, 20)**
Last Amateur Club: **Brampton Battalion (OHL)**

There is a new up-and-coming breed of defencemen in the game of hockey, and they are being classified as "hybrid" players. These players don't just park at the blue line and fire off slapshots, or stay behind to be the last guy back. In other words, they are not your typical stay-at-home defencemen. These players are strong both offensively and defensively, and most of them have played forward at some point in their career so they know how to rush and are not afraid to get close to the net. They're not shy, nor do they think it's wrong to let one of their teammates sit for a bit on the blue line while they move forward with the puck. They like to rush; they're good at rushing.

Brent Burns is a great example of a true hybrid.

Burns is extremely strong both offensively and defensively, can play defence and wing. The Hockey Canada management staff is looking very seriously at this kind of player. He may be known as a defenceman in the NHL, but when he played in the OHL for the Brampton Battalion, Brent Burns played right wing. In the 2003 NHL entry draft, Burns went as a forward in the first round and twentieth overall to the Minnesota Wild.

When he reported to training camp, Minnesota Wild coach Jacques Lemaire took one look at Burn's 6'5", 219 pound frame and decided that this young player might possibly be better as a defenceman. Size is a factor on the line. Lemaire is known in the hockey world to be a defensively minded coach so this was not a shock to anyone that he was willing to rework a player to suit his coaching style. In the 2003-04 season, Burns played as a defenceman in 36 games for the Wild. Although he was positioned

Brent Burns playing in the 2003 IIHF World Junior Championship in Halifax. Canada won the silver medal.

Idols:
**Lance Armstrong,
Mark Messier**

Favourite TV show:
Entourage

If not a hockey player would be a:
Green Beret

Person who had most influence on
hockey career growing up:
Dad

Best concert ever attended:
AC/DC

Most memorable minor
hockey experience:
**winning playoffs while
with the Marlies**

Favourite team growing up:
Toronto Maple Leafs

Favourite book:
Harry Potter series

Minnesota Wild

Brent Burns

2009 August orientation camp

on the blue line, he still possessed the natural offensive tendencies that he had learned as a winger. Often, he would flash forward and make big rushes from the blue line which worked and slotted him into the hybrid category.

Of course, the Hockey Canada staff also knows about his offensive skills because he played as a forward at the 2004 IIHF World Junior Championship in Finland. The team brought home a silver medal that year and Burns was a big part of Canada's win. He scored, picked up assists, and managed to take some heavy-duty penalties, labeling him as a physical force.

With the NHL lockout in 2004-05, Burns honed his defensive skills in the AHL and when the NHL resumed for the 2005-06 season he had a spot on the Wild as a defenceman. Taking his job seriously, he emerged as not only a goal scoring defenceman but also a tough player, getting into two big fights during the playoffs.

For the Hockey Canada management staff, Brent Burns sealed his position on the 2010 Olympic orientation-camp roster in 2008, when he played in the IIHF World Championships in Halifax. He was strong on the line and from a coaching standpoint, he was accountable, and he played well in every situation that was thrown his way. As a result, the IIHF Directorate voted him top defenceman for the tournament. This is the kind of player Hockey Canada is looking for as Steve Yzerman is big on trustworthiness at all times. The only downfall for Brent Burns during that tournament was the silver medal, as opposed to the coveted gold that the Canadian players love to win. To date, his Hockey Canada medals amount to two silvers.

Perhaps it is time for this new breed of hybrid player to bring home a gold medal. The playing style that got Burns invited to the orientation camp might be exactly what the 2010 roster needs.

Camp Highlights

Burns looked good, moving the puck well out of the zone. Paired with Bouwmeester, he did his job and looked as if he was the strong player he was two years ago when he was under the guidance of Jacques Lemaire.

2009 August orientation camp

Statistics– International								
Year	Team	Event	GP	G	A	PTS	PIM	Result
Regional								
Not applicable								
National								
2004	CAN	WJC	6	0	6	6	20	Silver
2008	CAN	WHC	9	3	6	9	16	Silver
	CAN	INTL TOTAL	15	3	12	15	36	
	CAN	SR TOTAL	9	3	6	9	16	

DREW DOUGHTY

DEFENCE #8

CANADA

Shoots: Right
Height: 6'1"
Weight: 203 lbs
Birthdate: December 8, 1989
Birthplace: London, Ont.
Hometown: London, Ont.
Team: Los Angeles Kings (NHL)
MHA: London MHA
NHL Draft: Los Angeles Kings: 2008 (1, 2)
Last Amateur Club: Guelph Storm (OHL)

Another member of the new breed of offensively-minded defencemen invited to camp is young gun Drew Doughty. Born on December 9, 1989, Drew Doughty was just 19 at the August orientation camp and will turn 20 during the 2010 Olympics.

Skilled offensively, Doughty likes to rush, and when given the opportunity he goes end-to-end. He is a creative player, and while he doesn't always score on his rushes, his calculated risk taking and bold moves will often put the puck in the opponents end to set up his team for a good scoring chance. At the same time, he works well defensively and frustrates his opposition by closing off ice space and controlling the puck to take precious seconds off the clock at the critical end of a penalty kill, a period, or a game. Plus, he does have an uncanny knack for creating scoring opportunities from the blue line.

Sounds like the perfect defensive package. When analyzed by the Hockey Canada management team they put him on the orientation-camp roster for a variety of reasons. They feel that for such a young player, he has tremendous composure and is "poised beyond his years." Doughty doesn't get rattled in the big games, which is so important when selecting members for an Olympic team because of the constant hype and media bombardment. It can be intense and unforgiving, and players need to be mentally and physically tough enough to survive both the criticism, and the compliments without it impacting their level of play. The management team also liked the fact that Doughty is extremely patient with the puck and waits for the right moment to make his pass. Such a talent and mindset is extremely important in international competition as the skilled European opposition prey on

Image provided by Aaron Bell/OHL

Drew Doughty grew up in London, Ontario, playing his Junior career in his home province. Here he is with the OHL's Guelph Storm.

Home Ice

Hockey hero:
Wayne Gretzky

Favourite TV show:
Entourage

Favourite activity outside of hockey:
going to the cottage

If not a hockey player would be a:
soccer player

Person who had most influence on
hockey career growing up:
parents

Best concert ever attended:
Keith Urban

Most memorable minor
hockey experience:
**winning All-Ontario in
Major Bantam**

Favourite team growing up:
Los Angeles Kings

2009 August orientation camp

Drew Doughty

CANADA

players that gamble with the puck and are quick to punish a careless pass up the middle and turnover with a surprise scoring chance.

Doughty was just drafted in 2008, and he went in the first round, second overall to the Los Angeles Kings. Prior to his arrival into the NHL, Doughty played for three years on the Guelph Storm in the Ontario Hockey League (OHL). As a 15-year-old, in 2005-06, Doughty managed to finish his rookie year with 33 points, (five goals and 28 assists) earning him a spot with the top-twenty rookie scorers in the OHL. And to top that off, he was the second highest scoring rookie defenceman in the entire OHL. Not bad for a kid who should have been still playing Midget hockey because of his young age. Even so, he led all of his Guelph defence teammates in scoring.

The next year, playing with the Storm, he continued his offensive/defensive playing style and ended up with 74 points (21 goals and 53 assists), to lead his team in the scoring race. Ending up second in points and assists in the OHL, and in the top five for goals, Doughty was named to the Western Conference All-Star Team for the OHL All-Star Classic.

Los Angeles Kings

Although he's young, he can still be classified as experienced, especially when it comes to international play. Doughty started playing for Team Canada at the 2006 Memorial of Ivan Hlinka in Slovakia/Czech Republic, giving him his first taste of what it feels like to win a gold medal. From there, he was named alternate captain for Canada's National Under-18 Team at the 2007 IIHF World Under-18 Championship in Finland, where they came fourth. When the idea for the Canada/Russia Super Series came to fruition in the fall of 2007, Hockey Canada snapped Doughty up, knowing that he was a player they wanted on the blue line.

The biggest and brightest moment in Doughty's international career came in 2008 when Canada's National Junior Team won the gold medal in the Czech Republic and he was named top defenceman of the tournament. In 2009, Doughty made the jump to play with the big boys and secured a spot on the Men's World Championship Team, travelling to Switzerland and playing in a heart-breaking, gold-medal round, where Canada lost to Russia and came home with the silver medal.

Drew Doughty is a young and extremely talented hockey player who has some of the essential skills that the Hockey Canada management team think are necessary ingredients for their blue line. The fact that he is experienced in international play also holds weight.

Camp Highlights

For a 19-year-old, Doughty had a phenomenal camp. He showed up to play and wasn't intimidated by the more experienced veterans. He made it known that he was in awe being on the ice with some of his hockey idols. In his first practice he was paired with Chris Pronger and he said, "that was pretty amazing." For the final game he was on Team White and was paired with Regehr.

Drew made his debut with the Senior Men's Team by playing at the 2009 IIHF Men's World Championship. Here, he is in possession of the puck. Canada won the silver medal.

		Statistics– **International**						
Year	Team	Event	GP	G	A	PTS	PIM	Result
		Regional						
2006	ONT	WU17	5	1	3	4	4	5th
		National						
2006	CAN	SU18	4	0	3	3	6	Gold
2007	CAN	WU18	6	2	3	5	8	4th
2007	CAN	SuperSeries	8	0	2	2	4	1st
2008	CAN	WJC	7	0	4	4	0	Gold
2009	CAN	WHC	9	1	6	7	4	Silver
	CAN	INTL TOTAL	37	3	18	21	22	
	CAN	SR TOTAL	9	1	6	7	4	

Drew Doughty

MIKE GREEN

DEFENCE #52

Shoots: **Right**
Height: **6'2"**
Weight: **208 lbs**
Birthdate: **October 12, 1985**
Birthplace: **Calgary, Alta.**
Hometown: **Calgary, Alta.**
Team: **Washington Capitals (NHL)**
MHA: **Hockey Calgary MHA**
NHL Draft/: **Washington Capitals: 2004 (1, 29)**
Last Amateur Club: **Saskatoon Blades (WHL)**

The Hockey Canada management team picked another offensively talented player when they put Mike Green's name on the orientation-camp roster. In the past few years, Green has emerged as a tremendously smart player who sees the ice really well. Like Doughty, he has great patience with the puck. He also has an understanding of the game and each player's position, so he often foresees a teammate's move in advance, and puts the puck into play when he knows his forwards are ready to break out. Organizers say he is a "great shot" and a dominant force with his team on the power play. These are all strong enough qualities for him to be invited to camp.

For five full seasons, Green played Major Junior with the Saskatoon Blades of the Western Hockey League (WHL). In his final season (2003-04), during his draft year, he recorded 14 goals for a total of 39 points. This offence, and his smart playing ability, got him drafted in the first round, twenty-ninth overall to the Washington Capitals.

Like many young players, Green played the up and down game, going between the NHL and the AHL. During the time that he moved from the Hershey Bears to the Washington Capitals, he kept honing his skills. His first goal in the NHL was scored against a typically stingy Ed Belfour on February 3, 2006, when the Washington Capitals were up against the Toronto Maple Leafs. His tenaciousness worked to get him selected to play in the 2007 NHL Young Stars Game for the Eastern Conference and, even with a hurt foot, he managed to pick up three assists.

Mike Green played minor hockey in Calgary, Alberta. Here he is playing for NASA.

Image provided by Nate Ewell of the Washington Capitals

Favourite movie:
The Hangover

If not a hockey player would be a:
Musician

Person who had most influence on
hockey career growing up:
Dave Smith (coach)

Best concert ever attended:
Metallica

Favourite band:
Seether

Most memorable minor
hockey experience:
**won provincials with
Simons Valley**

Hockey hero:
Scott Niedermayer

Favourite magazine:
Maxim

2009 August orientation camp

Mike Green

But Mike Green's big breakout year came in 2007-08, when he found himself playing for the Washington Capitals behind some great, young players like Alex Ovechkin, Alexander Semin and Nicklas Backstrom. Green rose to the challenge of playing with such talented players and emerged as an elite NHL defenceman, gaining the attention of Hockey Canada management and an invitation to the 2010 camp. It took until Thanksgiving for Green to find his stride, but when he did, he pounced on it, and made some big offensive plays, so much so that at the end of the season he had scored four game-winning goals. This made him a popular player with play-by-play announcers and fans alike as they nicknamed him "Game Over." His game winning goals were always in the last few minutes of the third period or in overtime. The Capitals made the playoffs for the first time since 2003 that season, and Green was certainly one of the reasons they were so successful.

Experience is something that the Hockey Canada management team reviews during their closed-door meetings. Green's international experience certainly wouldn't fill a full page or even a paragraph but he has a few lines beside his name. While Green didn't play for Canada's World Junior Team, he did play, and win a gold medal, for the Men's Under-18 Team at the 2003 IIHF World Under-18 Championship. Five years later, in 2008, he played on the IIHF World Championship Team when Canada hosted the tournament in Quebec City and Halifax. Unfortunately, Canada lost to Russia in the gold medal game but Mike Green was named to the tournament All-Star Team. Named as one of the best defencemen in the World Championships in 2008, the Team Canada management staff looked carefully at Mike Green during the 2008-09 season. Early in the season, however, injuries set him back a few games. Once he was back on the ice, he didn't waste any time showing his offensive skills. He managed to pick up back-to-back NHL Third Stars of the Weeks. Then in January and February, Green scored in eight consecutive games setting an NHL record for most consecutive games with a goal by a defenceman by beating Mike O'Connell's record in the 1983-84 NHL season.

Patience with the puck, a great shot, and fantastic offensive skills have earned Mike Green a spot on this coveted roster.

Camp Highlights
Green was paired with Duncan Keith and played on Team White. They were a positive pair and played a consistently good game. Green was good offensively, adding the odd rush to his game.

Washington Capitals

CANADA

2009 August orientation camp

Statistics– **International**

Year	Team	Event	GP	G	A	PTS	PIM	Result
		Regional						
2002	PAC	WU17						
		National						
2002	CAN	SU18	5	0	2	2	2	Gold
2003	CAN	WU18	7	0	0	0	2	Gold
2009	CAN	WHC	9	4	8	12	2	Silver
	CAN	INTL TOTAL	21	4	10	14	6	
	CAN	SR TOTAL	9	4	8	12	2	

Mike Green

DAN HAMHUIS

DEFENCE #2

Shoots: **Left**
Height: **6'1"**
Weight: **203 lbs**
Birthdate: **December 13, 1982**
Birthplace: **Smithers, B.C.**
Hometown: **Smithers, B.C.**
Team: **Nashville Predators (NHL)**
MHA: **Smithers MHA**
NHL Draft: **Nashville Predators: 2001 (1, 12)**
Last Amateur Club: **Prince George Cougars (WHL)**

Some great descriptions for the new breed of defenceman are flashy, rushing, goal scorer. This kind of defenceman makes everyone sit on the edge of their seat, take notice, and say wow. But what about the guy who is considered to be consistent and dependable? Do these skills get noticed in the new and fast style of hockey that is being played today? Obviously, yes, because these were the words the Hockey Canada management team used when they described Dan Hamhuis. They said he was "dependable, consistent and that his play doesn't jump around," and that on a "nightly basis he is just so reliable." Plus, he is a sound positional defensive player. They also feel that Hamhuis is someone who, when he steps on the ice, can stabilize everyone he plays with. *That* is a true skill. If all the defencemen chosen for this team are offensive and like to rush, then who is left to hold down the fort? Guys like Dan Hamhuis do that job.

Hamhuis is the guy a coach can go to when it's time for the second-unit power play. The coaches yell down the bench, Hamhuis jumps, skates to position and does his job, no questions asked. Over the past few years with the Nashville Predators, Hamhuis has emerged as a strong contender for Team Canada.

Hamhuis wasn't always so defensively minded. He played his Junior career with the Prince George Cougars, taking a place on their roster for four years where he consistently scored and picked up his fair share of assists. In 2001 he was drafted to the Nashville Predators, going twelfth in the first round because of these scoring skills, though like many, he too remained in Junior hockey before joining his NHL team to further develop his skills. In 2001-02,

Everyone has to start somewhere. Here, Dan Hamhuis is just learning how to stand up on skates. He played for Smithers, B.C., minor hockey.

2009 August orientation camp

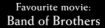

Favourite movie:
Band of Brothers

Favourite activity outside hockey:
camping

If not a hockey player would be a:
general contractor

Person who had most influence on
hockey career growing up:
Dad

Favourite band:
Bruce Springstein

Most memorable experience
since being pro:
**winning provincial
Bantam A Championship**

Hockey hero:
Trevor Linden

Favourite book:
The Bourne Series

Dan Hamhuis

2009 August orientation camp

his final year with the Cougars, and as the captain of the team, he registered 10 goals and 50 assists for a total of 60 points. At that time in his career, he had some good offensive skills, which helped him win player of the year in the WHL.

When Hamhuis made the leap to the NHL, he realized immediately that the game was faster than the Juniors, the boys were bigger and stronger, and he would have to make some adjustments to keep up. Positioning became his focus. In Junior hockey he could be a little out of position, get to the puck on time, and still make the play, but in the big leagues he understood that being out of position meant being out of the play and putting his team in jeopardy. In hockey lingo, he would get burned! Pro players would be there to scald him good, so he decided to concentrate on defence and let the offence come when the time was right. That first year in the pros, Hamhuis set a personal goal to just learn the basics of pro hockey and not try to be too flashy or too offensive. By doing that, he has become known as a tremendous positional player.

Hamhuis went to orientation camp with a lot of international experience. He is a proud Canadian and never turns down the opportunity to play for Team Canada when Hockey Canada seeks players for the Men's World Championships each spring. For four consecutive years, (2006, 2007, 2008, 2009) Hamhuis has won two silvers and a gold medal in that tournament. The gold came in 2007, when the team travelled to Russia. This experience gave him a taste of what it is like to win gold and an understanding of how hard a team has to work to make that happen. Hamhuis was also a strong member of the Canadian Junior Team, having played in 2001 and 2002. In total, he has played for Canada in six international tournaments.

Dan Hamhuis is a player with tremendous international experience. He is a solid, dependable player that is consistent and reliable night after night.

Camp Highlights

Hamhuis didn't let anyone down at the camp. Paired with Robidas on Team Red, Hamhuis played his safe game. He didn't back down from anyone and played as if he thought he was bigger than most of the guys on the ice.

Nashville Predators

Year	Team	Event	GP	G	A	PTS	PIM	Result
Statistics– International								
Regional								
1999	BC	CWG	unavailable					Bronze
National								
2001	CAN	WJC	7	0	1	1	8	Bronze
2002	CAN	WJC	6	0	3	3	8	Bronze
2006	CAN	WHC	9	1	4	5	10	4th
2007	CAN	WHC	9	1	2	3	2	Gold
2008	CAN	WHC	9	1	1	2	8	Silver
2009	CAN	WHC	9	2	2	4	16	Silver
	CAN	INTL TOTAL	49	5	13	18	52	
	CAN	SR TOTAL	36	5	9	14	36	

Dan Hamhuis

DUNCAN KEITH

DEFENCE #2

Shoots: **Left**
Height: **6'1"**
Weight: **194 lbs**
Birthdate: **July 16, 1983**
Birthplace: **Winnipeg, Man.**
Hometown: **Penticton, B.C.**
Team: **Chicago Blackhawks (NHL)**
MHA: **Penticton MHA**
NHL Draft: **Chicago Blackhawks: 2002 (2, 54)**
Last Amateur Club: **Kelowna Rockets (WHL)**

nother strong defending defenceman is Duncan Keith. The Hockey Canada management team feels that Keith has somewhat of the unknown factor, though he's worked hard and strived to make himself noticed. Ken Hitchcock sees some Hamhuis in him, and Kevin Lowe compares him to a possible up-and-coming Scott Niedermayer. Hockey Canada maintains very detailed information on each potential player for Canada's international teams and in Duncan Keith's binder the phrase, "extremely smart positional player" is the tag line that accompanies his profile. The Hockey Canada management team like that Keith has "very effective mobility." Quick on his feet, he can move to the puck, change directions and clear the zone effectively. He's steady, solid, and provides his team with impressive defence without a lot of flash or rushing to the net.

Duncan Keith grew up in Penticton, B.C., and played his Junior A hockey with the Penticton Panthers.

Like his on-ice playing, Keith's career to date has seen steady improvement while on his rise to the top. Most fans will remember his breakout year as the 2006-07 season with the Chicago Blackhawks, though he logged many years of hard work to get to that point in his career and receive an invite to this Olympic orientation camp.

He is a player who had a vision, and who persistently worked hard to make his dream come true.

Playing most of his minor hockey years in Penticton, British Columbia, Duncan Keith didn't stray too far from home when he decided to try the Junior A route. His first gig was as a 16-year-old in the BCJHL playing for the Penticton Panthers. This afforded Keith the opportunity to stay at home with his parents and

Idols:
Parents

Biggest pet peeve:
second-hand smoke

Hockey Hero:
Pavel Bure

Favourite movie:
Braveheart

Favourite activities
outside of hockey:
music, boating

Favourite band:
Rolling Stones

Favourite team growing up:
Winnipeg Jets

Favourite book:
Monster

2009 August orientation camp

Duncan Keith

CANADA

continue to attend his jurisdiction high school. Upon graduation, Keith chose to take the NCAA route instead of the Major Juniors, accepting a scholarship to Michigan State University.

When the time came for the World Junior Selection Camp in 2001-02, Keith was one of 38 invitees. The Hockey Canada scouts had been watching him play College Hockey and liked what they saw. In the end, when the final team roster was named, Duncan Keith did not make the cut. Instead of playing for Canada, he spent the Christmas holidays watching the World Juniors on television.

While still at Michigan State, Keith was drafted by the Chicago Blackhawks in the 2002 entry draft. Fall arrived, and once again, Keith packed his bags for college. After his second year, however, Keith made the decision to return to Okanagan and play for the Kelowna Rockets. In just 37 games with the Rockets, he earned 46 points (11 goals and 35 assists) and he put together the amazing plus/minus stat of +32.

Scouts took notice and the Chicago Blackhawks signed Keith to a contract. It wasn't until 2005 before Keith actually played in the NHL. In his two years in the minors, he made a name for himself as the guy who was a great shutdown defenceman that could carry heavy minutes of ice time. His debut NHL game was on October 5, 2005.

Once in the NHL, Keith continued to be a heavy minute guy with a great plus/minus average. In 2005-06 he averaged 23 minutes in 81 games. Then in 2006-07 he played 82 games and became the team leader in minutes played, averaging 23 minutes a game. Tough with no fear, Keith also recorded a whooping 148 blocked shots. By January in the 2007-08 season, Keith had upped his playing time and was logging 24:31 minutes of ice time while holding a +14 plus/minus.

The Hockey Canada management team really noticed Keith in 2008, when he played in the IIHF Men's World Championship in Halifax. He was definitely a dominating force on the blue line and a strong, solid defenceman.

This accountability earned this "unknown" a berth on the orientation camp roster. In this business unknowns are always the ones to be watched.

2009 August orientation camp

Chicago Blackhawks

Camp Highlights

Efficient and intelligent were two words that were used to describe how Duncan Keith played during the camp and in the Red and White game. He was paired with Mike Green on Team White and they were definitely a good match.

		Statistics– **International**						
Year	Team	Event	GP	G	A	PTS	PIM	Result
		Regional						
2000	PAC	WU17	6	1	3	4	0	Bronze
		National						
2008	CAN	WHC	9	0	2	2	6	Silver
	CAN	INTL TOTAL	9	0	2	2	6	
	CAN	SR TOTAL	9	0	2	2	6	

SCOTT NIEDERMAYER

DEFENCE #27

CANADA

Shoots : **Left**
Height: **6'1"**
Weight: **200 lbs**
Birthdate: **September 31, 1973**
Birthplace: **Edmonton, Alta.**
Hometown: **Cranbrook, B.C.**
Team: **Anaheim Ducks (NHL)**
MHA: **Cranbrook MHA**
NHL Draft: **New Jersey Devils: 1991 (1, 3)**
Last Amateur Club: **Kamloops Blazers (WHL)**

Fast, skilled, solid on the blue line, but also likes to rush offensively, Scott Niedermayer is a definite contender for the 2010 team. The Hockey Canada management team is well aware of Niedermayer's competitiveness and they admire his drive to win the gold.

This Niedermayer brother has debated retirement from the game the past few years. In a telephone call in the spring, he guaranteed the management team for Hockey Canada that, yes, he definitely wanted to play on the Olympic Team. Wearing the red and white Canadian jersey is something he is proud of doing and would want to do again if given the opportunity. But he did say he had to do what was best for his family and for his NHL team. Not long after that conversation, he signed on with the Anaheim Ducks for another one-year contract. This, coupled with his verbal agreement to Hockey Canada, demonstrated that he's not ready to hang up his skates just yet, and showed a commitment to his career and to the sport of hockey.

It is not known if this will be Scott's last year or not. At this point, no one knows the answer to that—not even Scott. He has enjoyed an incredible career, and it is apparent that he is again prepared to give his all to play on Canada's Olympic Team, with hopes of winning gold on home turf. With this goal ahead, he was put on the roster as a strong defensive contender.

Although Scott was born in Edmonton, he was raised, and played his minor hockey career, in Cranbrook, British Columbia, and played his Major Junior career in Kamloops for the Blazers. Scott is no stranger to Olympic competition but the opportunity of

Image provided by Hockey Canada

Scott Niedermayer has been with Team Canada for many years. This photo is from his first year when he played for the 1991 IIHF World Junior Championship Team.

Hockey hero:
Paul Coffey

Favourite movie:
Braveheart

Favourite activities
outside of hockey:
hiking, camping

Person who had most influence on
hockey career growing up:
Parents

Favourite band:
Pearl Jam

Most memorable minor
hockey experience:
**winning provincial
championship in Peewee
and Bantam**

Favourite team growing up:
New York Islanders

Favourite magazine:
Explore

2009 August orientation camp

Scott Niedermayer

playing at the 2010 Games is particularly meaningful to him given his connection to British Columbia and the feeling that he'd be playing near his hometown.

Scott was named to the 2006 Olympic team but was sidelined for injuries and didn't travel to Turin with the team. Scott was also named to the 2002 Olympic team and was a proud member of the Canadian team that won an Olympic gold medal at the Games in Salt Lake City. His experience sits high on the list with the management and coaching staff. Plus, Scott is a natural born leader and one of the best skaters in the league. Looking at his complete package of talents and skills, he would definitely make an attractive addition to the 2010 team.

But let's backtrack and talk about his experience. Not only does Niedermayer have an Olympic gold medal, but he is the only Canadian (and only player in the history of hockey) with six major championships to his credit. Niedermayer has experience that no other player in hockey has. These major championships being the Stanley Cup, Memorial Cup, IIHF World Junior Ice Hockey Championship gold medal, Olympic gold medal, World Cup of Hockey title, and IIHF Men's World Ice Hockey Championship gold medal.

It was after his Stanley Cup victory on June 19, 2007 that he made his first announcement that perhaps he should retire from this game. With such a list of accomplishments, had he felt that there was nothing left to win?

Again, on July 1, 2007, he reiterated that he was thinking of retiring.

Because he didn't make his decision, the Anaheim Ducks suspended him for salary-cap reasons. Then in the fall he opted out of training camp because he was still undecided. His

Anaheim Ducks

'C' was taken from him and he didn't play that season until the Ducks were 28 games into their schedule. On December 5, 2007, he returned to play the remainder of the season.

Fast-forward to 2009-2010. Scott is still playing Canada's great sport and has repeatedly given his verbal word that he wants to be involved with Hockey Canada and be a part of the Olympic Team. He is a highly skilled player who has experience and would be a most welcome addition to the team if he is on his game.

Camp Highlights

Niedermayer showed off his amazing talents at the camp and during the Red and White game. He played for Team Red with Shea Weber and their unique skills complimented each other making for a lethal combination. Niedermayer was the skater on the tandem and showed amazing finesse and brainpower.

2009 August orientation camp

Year	Team	Event	GP	G	A	PTS	PIM	Result
		Statistics– **International**						
		Regional						
1990	PAC	QUE U17			unavailable			n/a
		National						
1991	CAN	WJC	7	0	0	0	0	Gold
1992	CAN	WJC	7	0	0	0	10	6th
1996	CAN	WC	8	1	3	4	6	2nd
2002	CAN	OLY	6	1	1	2	4	Gold
2004	CAN	WHC	9	3	2	5	12	Gold
2004	CAN	WC	6	1	1	2	9	1st
	CAN	INTL TOTAL	43	6	7	13	41	
	CAN	SR TOTAL	29	6	7	13	31	

DION PHANEUF

DEFENCE #3

Shoots: **Left**
Height: **6'3"**
Weight: **214 lbs**
Birthdate: **April 10, 1985**
Birthplace: **Edmonton, Alta.**
Hometown: **Edmonton, Alta.**
Team: **Calgary Flames (NHL)**
MHA: **South Side Athletic Club MHA**
NHL Draft: **Calgary Flames: 2003 (1, 9)**
Last Amateur Club: **Red Deer Rebels (WHL)**

Known as one of the hardest-hitting, glass-rattling, defencemen in the NHL, Dion Phaneuf could certainly add great toughness to Canada's blue line. The Hockey Canada management team used the word "reckless" to describe Phaneuf, but they used it in a good way. This recklessness gives him an edge and keeps his opponents on their toes for lack of knowing what he will do next. And sometimes that next thing is a crushing hit into the boards. This makes him an intimidating player. The opposition is well aware of his actions, understanding he is a huge, physical threat. He also has the ability to score now and again.

It may be Phaneuf's first time playing in the Olympic Games but it certainly is not his first time wearing a Team Canada jersey. Phaneuf travelled overseas to Helsinki, Finland with the 2004 World Junior team. At the time he was 19 years old and playing in the WHL for the Red Deer Rebels. That year, Canada won a silver medal, losing to the U.S. Devastated with the loss, Phanuef's only consolation was being named to the tournament All-Star Team.

In 2005, he once again donned the Canadian jersey when the Canadian World Junior Team went to Grand Forks, North Dakota. Canada made it to the gold medal round where they faced their rival, Russia. The NHL lockout had certainly helped the Canadian teams as many young juniors who should have been playing in the NHL were now eligible to play for Team Canada.

The Russians kept pace, playing with the Canadian team for only the first 20 minutes of the game, after which Canada stepped up the intensity and went on to win 6-1. Dominant on the blue line during the entire tournament, Phaneuf's 6'3" presence stood

Dion Phaneuf grew up in Edmonton, Alberta, and played most of his minor hockey career with the South Side Athletic Club.

Hockey hero:
Wayne Gretzky

Favourite TV show:
Nip Tuck

Favourite activities
outside of hockey:
movies, music

If not a hockey player would be a:
lawyer

Person who had most influence on
hockey career growing up:
Dad

Favourite band:
Tragically Hip

Favourite team growing up:
Edmonton

Favourite magazine:
Dupont Registry

2009 August orientation camp

Dion Phaneuf

CANADA

2009 August orientation camp

solid, never wavering. He kept many of his opposing players at bay because they were just too nervous to go near him for fear of being hammered against the boards. For the second year in a row, Phaneuf was named to the tournament All-Star Team and named Top Defenceman of the tournament. In this tournament, Phaneuf showed what he was truly made of. When Team Canada played the Czech Republic in the semifinal game of the tournament, Phaneuf laid a hit so hard against Rostislav Olesz, that Olesz left the ice and didn't play the rest of the tournament due to a concussion. The word was out—this kid could hit hard and this intimidated opponents.

Phaneuf attended the 2003 NHL Draft on a high, and was drafted ninth overall in the first round by the Calgary Flames. He didn't make the leap to the NHL right away and stayed with the Red Deer Rebels. It was a smart move because in 2004 Phaeuf won the Bill Hunter Memorial Trophy for the WHL's Defenceman of the year, and was also named to the CHL First All-Star Team.

Just when it was time for Phaneuf to make his NHL debut, the NHL decided to go ahead with their lockout. Phaneuf headed back to Red Deer for another season of WHL hockey. Again that year he won the WHL Bill Hunter Memorial Trophy for top defenceman.

Finally, the big moment came and on October 5, 2005. Phaneuf played in his first NHL game, one that Calgary dropped to Minnesota 6-3. Just five days later, Phaneuf scored his first goal in a game against the Colorado Avalanche. He also picked up an assist that game.

It didn't take him long to become one of the Flames' top players. In November of that year, he was named Rookie of the Month and was being ranked third rookie in the league—right behind superstars Alex Ovechkin and Sidney Crosby. That fuelled his fire, and at the NHL awards banquet in June of 2006, Phaneuf was a finalist for the Calder Cup Trophy for the NHL's Rookie of the Year. Alex Ovechkin won.

It was no surprise to anyone when during the NHL All-Star break in 2007 that he was also voted the league's hardest hitter in an ESPN informal poll of 141 NHL players. Phaneuf played in the NHL All-Star game and he scored the longest empty-net goal in All-Star history. He was behind his own net and banked the shot off the boards, like a perfect pool shot, and it rolled into the empty Eastern net.

Phaneuf has also played senior hockey for Canada. After missing the first two games of the 2007 IIHF Men's World Tournament, Phaneuf flew to Russia as a late addition. The Canadian team welcomed Phaneuf and he settled in to play hard, fast-paced international hockey. Canada dominated the tournament and came home with the gold medal.

If picked for this prestigious Olympic team, Dion Phanuef will have to add some of that reckless toughness that is his signature on the blue line. Hockey Canada will be watching him intently when the 2009-10 NHL season begins, with the hope that he continues to play his style of game, a style that would benefit Team Canada.

Camp Highlights

Because of his hard-hitting playing style, the Red and White inter-squad game didn't necessarily show off all of Phaneuf's talents. Teamed with Seabrook, he had to tone down his crushing hits. Fortunately, the management team knows this, and will watch him in the fall of 2009.

Calgary Flames

	Statistics– **International**							
Year	Team	Event	GP	G	A	PTS	PIM	Result
		Regional						
2002	PAC	WU17	6	3	5	8	8	Silver
		National						
2002	CAN	SU18	5	1	1	2	4	Gold
2004	CAN	WJC	6	2	2	4	29	Silver
2005	CAN	WJC	6	1	5	6	14	Gold
2007	CAN	WHC	7	0	8	8	2	Gold
	CAN	INTL TOTAL	24	4	16	20	49	
	CAN	SR TOTAL	7	0	8	8	2	

Dion Phaneuf

CHRIS PRONGER

DEFENCE #20

Shoots: **Left**
Height: **6'6"**
Weight : **213 lbs**
Birthdate: **October 10, 1974**
Birthplace: **Dryden, Ont.**
Hometown: **Dryden, Ont.**
Team: **Philadelphia Flyers (NHL)**
MHA: **Dryden MHA**
NHL Draft: **Hartford Whalers: 1993 (1, 2)**
Last Amateur Club: **Peterborough Petes (OHL)**

At 6'6", Chris Pronger has the longest reach of any of the defencemen chosen for this roster. This, coupled with a host of other important attributes, makes him an effective player. He has a great first pass and tremendous patience with the puck, plus the ability to log big minutes in almost any game situation. In Hockey Canada lingo he is, "effective in any situation."

Has he had his share of ups and downs? Sure he has. But he's also been in the game a long time. One advantage Pronger has in this upcoming Olympics is that the tournament is being played on the smaller North American sized ice surface, as opposed to what is typically seen in international hockey. The Hockey Canada management team knows that the tighter playing area is where Pronger thrives.

Pronger has been playing for eons it seems, and is one of the veterans to this game, especially to international hockey. With a career as long as Pronger's, ups and downs are to be expected, he is human after all. Pronger was born in 1974, which will make him 36 years old at the 2010 Olympic Games. The only defenceman older than him at camp was Scott Niedermayer, and only by one year.

As a young player, Pronger was always good. Drafted by the Peterborough Petes when he was a bantam, he had two stellar seasons with them, racking up both points and penalties. He quickly became known as the defenceman with speed, and scouts ranked him high for the draft. In the 1993 NHL entry draft, as expected, Pronger went second overall to the Hartford Whalers. Only the Russian superstar, Alexandre Daigle, went ahead of him.

Chris Pronger, at 18, playing for the 1993 IIHF World Junior Championship Team.

Nickname:
Prongs

Organization/Charity support:
Different Orange County charities. Sat on the board of Children's Hospital St. Louis. Active with The Children's Miracle Network

Favourite activities outside of hockey:
golf, boating, fishing

Hockey Hero:
Mike Bossy

Favourite team growing up:
New York Islanders

Minor Hockey Association:
Dryden MHA

Philadelphia Flyers

Chris Pronger

CANADA

In his first season with the Whalers, Pronger managed to make it to the NHL All-Rookie Team.

From Hartford, Pronger went to St. Louis and his career with them lasted nine years. After the lockout, he was traded to the Edmonton Oilers for one year before being traded to the Anaheim Ducks. The move proved to be good for Pronger. It was with Anaheim that he and his team won the Stanley Cup in 2007–08.

Pronger is one of the very few players on the orientation-camp roster who has played in three Olympic Games (1998, 2002, and 2006). In 1998 at the age of 24, he played with the iconic Wayne Gretzky. But his roots with Team Canada didn't start with that Olympics. His first foray into international hockey was in 1993 when he played in the IIHF World Junior Championship in Gavel, Sweden, winning a gold medal. To put this in perspective, fellow player, Drew Doughty who was born in 1989, was all of three years old when Pronger arrived home with an international gold medal around his neck. Many of the other defencemen at the orientation camp were also just learning to skate and starting their minor hockey careers when Pronger was already playing in an international competition, and winning medals.

In between Pronger's first international competition in 1993, and the last time he graced the big ice in Turin, Italy at the 2006 Winter Olympics, he has been involved in four other international championships. Most memorable was the 2002 Winter Olympics in Salt Lake City when the team won gold and Pronger was named an alternate captain.

Pronger is just one of a handful of players that has captained two different NHL teams: the St. Louis Blues and the Anaheim Ducks. Pronger played in his 1000th NHL game on February 20, 2009.

2009 August orientation camp

Okay, so he has experience and, yes, he has skill. What Hockey Canada will be looking for when considering him for the 2010 team is that same level of energy and passion that he has demonstrated throughout his career.

Veteran vs. rookie? That seems to be the question that the Hockey Canada management team is asking when selecting members for the upcoming Olympics. They've obviously picked both kinds of players to attend camp for a reason. They need veteran players to lead this team and with all of Pronger's experience and success, he will definitely receive consideration for a spot on the team.

Camp Highlights

Great camp, great game for Pronger. Pronger definitely plays better on the left side so the pairing with Dan Boyle worked for him. They definitely complemented each other. He looked strong, and played like a true, experienced veteran.

Chris was a member of the 2006 Winter Olympic Team that travelled to Turin, Italy. The veterans from that team are anxious to make the 2010 team, hoping to prove Canada can win the gold.

Statistics– International

Year	Team	Event	GP	G	A	PTS	PIM	Result
			Regional					
1991	ONT	U17	unavailable					n/a
			National					
1991	CAN	SU18	6	3	4	7	16	2nd
1993	CAN	WJC	7	1	3	4	6	Gold
1997	CAN	WHC	9	0	2	2	10	Gold
1998	CAN	OLY	6	0	0	0	4	4th
2002	CAN	OLY	6	0	1	1	2	Gold
2006	CAN	OLY	6	1	2	3	16	7th
	CAN	INTL TOTAL	40	5	12	17	54	
	CAN	SR TOTAL	27	1	5	6	32	

Chris Pronger

ROBYN REGEHR

DEFENCE #28

Shoots: **Left**
Height: **6'3"**
Weight: **225 lbs**
Birthdate: **April 19, 1980**
Birthplace: **Recife, Brazil**
Hometown: **Rosthern, Sask.**
Team: **Calgary Flames (NHL)**
MHA: **Rosthern MHA**
NHL Draft: **Colorado Avalanche: 1998 (1, 19)**
Last Amateur Club: **Kamloops Blazers (WHL)**

CANADA

Funnily enough, when the Hockey Canada management team talked about Robyn Regehr they said he was, "good at keeping the group focused." This is something they didn't mention with any other player. Then they added that he was "a great leader." Like Pronger, they feel that he is a player who is more effective on the smaller ice surface. He makes good outlet passes and needs less room to regroup and help to get the forwards going. Of course, it was also noted that he is a great defending defenceman with a strong work ethic, and he plays his size all game long.

Much of Regehr's leadership qualities and positive attitude can be attributed to his ability to overcome hardship and cope in a challenging situation. Regehr had a different childhood; his parents were missionaries and he was born in the South American country of Brazil. From Brazil his family moved to the island of Java in Indonesia and Regehr was almost eight years old before his family returned to Canada and settled on a farm in Saskatchewan. While most young Canadian boys start playing hockey at the age of just four or five, Regehr started when he was eight. He had to work hard to catch up and by the time he was in his teens he knew he wanted to be a professional hockey player.

Regehr chose the Major Junior route, playing for the Kamloops Blazers for three years. He quickly became known as a talented defenceman, and went nineteenth overall to the Colorado Avalanche in the 1998 NHL Entry Draft. In his last year with the Kamloops Blazers he had turned into a physical player and was named an all-star.

Image provided by Sean Kelso of the Calgary Flames

Robyn Reghr played minor hockey in Saskatchewan with Rosthern Minor Hockey Association. Although he didn't start playing until he was eight, it didn't take him long to earn a "C" on his jersey.

Hockey heroes:
**Chris Chelios,
Larry Robinson**

Favourite TV show:
Ice Road Truckers

Favourite activities
outside of hockey:
sailing, fishing

If not a hockey player would be a:
farmer

Person who had most influence on
hockey career growing up:
Dad

Favourite band:
Motley Crue

Favourite book:
**The Spy Who Came
in from the Cold
by John Le Carre**

Favourite team growing up:
Montreal Canadiens

2009 August orientation camp

Robyn Regehr

CANADA

Regehr never played a game with the Avalanche as he was sent packing in a trade to the Calgary Flames on February 28, 1999. Regehr went to the Calgary Flames with Rene Corbet, Wade Belak and a draft pick, for Theoren Fleury and Chris Dingham. The Avalanche wanted a veteran sharpshooter to help them through a Stanley Cup run and they thought Fleury was going to help them get the job done.

Just when everything was going well for Regehr, tragedy struck. In the summer of 1999 Regehr was back in Saskatchewan training, farming, and enjoying summer with his friends when an oncoming car hit him in a head-on collison. The passengers of the other car died and 19-year-old Regehr went to the hospital with two fractured legs. With just two months until Calgary's training camp, Regehr devoted all his time to rehabilitation. His perseverance paid off and less than four months after his accident, on October 28, with screws in his legs, he made his NHL debut in a game against the Ottawa Senators. With only five real games under his belt since

2009 August orientation camp

the previous May, he played 15 minutes that game. Overall, Flames coach Brian Sutter was pleased with Regehr's performance. Regehr went on to play 57 games for the Flames that season.

Internationally, Regehr has experience. He started his international career, like most young players, in the World Juniors. He won a silver medal for Canada at the 1999 IIHF World Junior Championships in Winnipeg and in 2000 he made the jump and flew to Russia to play in the IIHF Men's World Championship, where they finished fourth. With no gold medal to speak of, Regehr managed to crack the 2004 World Cup Roster, winning a World Cup title. In 2005 he won a silver medal in Austria while playing on the Men's World Team and then in 2006 he earned a spot on the Olympic Team.

Regehr is one of those players who isn't too flashy, but he gets the job done. He is a defending defenceman with strong leadership qualities. Will that be enough to get him through to the next round? Sometimes perseverance pays off.

Camp Highlights

Regehr is part of the hard-hitting group of defencemen that the management staff and media called the Calgary contingency. It isn't fair to assess his play in the Red and White game because he wasn't allowed to show his true colours as the game was coined as a "friendly scrimmage." He will get a good look in the fall, when the Flames resume play.

Calgary Flames

Statistics– **International**								
Year	Team	Event	GP	G	A	PTS	PIM	Result
Regional								
1997	WEST	WU17	4	1	2	3	2	4th
National								
1997	CAN	SU18	--	--	--	--	--	Gold
1999	CAN	WJC	7	0	0	0	2	Silver
2000	CAN	WHC	6	0	0	0	2	4th
2004	CAN	WC	6	0	0	0	6	1st
2005	CAN	WHC	9	0	0	0	4	Silver
2006	CAN	OLY	6	0	1	1	2	7th
	CAN	INTL TOTAL	34	0	1	1	16	
	CAN	SR TOTAL	27	0	1	1	14	

STEPHANE ROBIDAS

DEFENCE #3

Shoots: **Right**
Height: **5'11"**
Weight: **190 lbs**
Birthdate: **March 3, 1977**
Birthplace: **Sherbrooke, QC**
Hometown: **Sherbrooke, QC**
Team: **Dallas Stars (NHL)**
MHA: **Magog MHA**
NHL Draft: **Montreal Canadiens: 1995 (7, 164)**
Last Amateur Club: **Shawinigan Cataractes (QMJHL)**

Ultra-competitive is an honest description of Stephane Robidas. No guts, no glory suits his playing style. In fact, in 2008-09 Robidas won the "No Guts, No Glory" contest form TSN, which is a yearly unofficial award given out to the toughest player in the NHL season. Robidas is 5'11", and weighs 10 pounds short of 200, yet those statistics puts him in the "small" category of defencemen named to this roster. That small category is a group of two with Dan Boyle being the other member. They are the only two defencemen whose height doesn't hit the six foot mark, and whose weight is around 190 pounds.

Even with his size disadvantage, Robidas is a fantastic one-on-one player. He also has great mobility on his skates and a good first pass. Robidas has had his fair share of injuries during his career, mostly from blocked shots and hits to the face, but he is the kind of player who will return to the ice with stitches—if the medical personnel will let him.

For the Hockey Canada management team, Robidas is a "feel-good selection." And can also be described as a "passionate long shot."

His road to the NHL was rather bumpy. In the 1995 Entry Draft, he went in the seventh round, a hundred and sixty-fifth overall to the Montreal Canadiens. Not exactly a stellar draft position. That didn't faze Robidas and he continued his Junior career in the QMJHL, getting named to their first All-Star Team two years running (1996, 1997). Then in 1997 he won the Emile Bouchard Trophy as the QMJHL's Defenceman of the Year.

When his Junior career was over, the Canadiens immediately sent him to the minors and he played with the Fredericton Canadiens for two years and the Quebec Citadelles for one.

Image provided by Jason Rademan of the Dallas Stars

Love the smile. Stephane Robidas grew up in Quebec and played his minor hockey career with the Magog Minor Hockey Association.

Home Ice

Hockey hero:
Mario Lemieux

Favourite TV show:
Prison Break

If not a hockey player would be a:
policeman

Favourite activity outside of
hockey:
boating

Person who had most influence on
hockey career growing up:
Dad

Favourite band:
Nickelback

Favourite team growing up:
Montreal Canadiens

Favourite magazine:
Men's Fitness

2009 August orientation camp

Stephane Robidas

Finally, he was called up to play with the Montreal Canadiens before they decided to put him on waivers. Robidas went on waivers just after the 2001-02 season where he had played 56 games and acquired 11 points (one goal and 10 assists), but he had a plus/minus of -25.

On October 4, 2002, in the waiver draft, Robidas was claimed by the Atlanta Thrashers who immediately dealt him like the top card on a deck to the Dallas Stars. During his first season with the Stars, he played 76 games but when the 2003-04 season rolled around, Robidas heard the rumours early in the fall. Time to pack his bags again. After just 14 games with Dallas he was sent to the Chicago Blackhawks where he finished the season playing 45 games. This time he managed 12 points and a +6 plus/minus.

The improvement in his stats didn't do him much good though. When the next season rolled around, the lockout had taken effect and Robidas packed his bags again and flew to Germany. The Europeans liked him and the fans took to his game right away. When the lockout was over, Robidas pondered staying in Germany. Since Chicago didn't qualify him, he became an unrestricted free agent, and, after all, it didn't look as if any NHL teams really wanted him.

At the tenth hour, he found a home back in North America with the Dallas Stars and the rest of his story, so far, has a happy ending. His "ultra competiveness" has created a space for him to emerge as a real talent. Here he is, just a few years later, a contender for the 2010 Olympic Team, being classified as one of the best defencemen in the NHL. His yo-yo career has made him tough.

Along with all his on-ice attributes, it has been noted by the Hockey Canada management team, that Robidas has two years of international experience. Robidas was a member of Team Canada at the 2001 IIHF World Championships, finishing fifth and at the 2006 IIHF World Championships, finishing fourth. He has yet to medal.

Dallas Stars

2009 August orientation camp

Many feel he has earned his way onto this roster by being tough, by skating hard, by working the puck out of the zone with that first pass, and by being, most importantly, ultra competitive. This player never backs down and never gives up.

Camp Highlights

Robidas didn't disappoint. He played a good game on the blue line. He was one of the players who "did what he was supposed to do." He was paired with Hamhuis and they played good, safe hockey together.

Statistics– **International**								
Year	Team	Event	GP	G	A	PTS	PIM	Result
Regional								
1994	QUE	WU17	-	-	-	-	-	Gold
National								
2001	CAN	WHC	7	0	1	1	0	5th
2006	CAN	WHC	9	1	1	2	6	4th
	CAN	INTL TOTAL	16	1	2	3	6	
	CAN	SR TOTAL	16	1	2	3	6	

Stephane Robidas

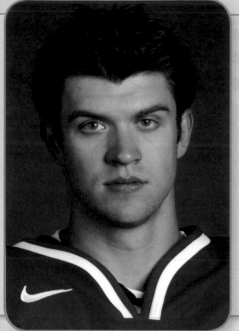

BRENT SEABROOK

DEFENCE #7

Shoots: **Right**
Height: **6'3"**
Weight: **220 lbs**
Birthdate: **April 20, 1985**
Birthplace: **Richmond, B.C.**
Hometown: **Tsawwassen, B.C.**
Team: **Chicago Blackhawks (NHL)**
MHA: **South Delta MHA**
NHL Draft: **Chicago Blackhawks: 2003 (1, 14)**
Last Amateur Club: **Lethbridge Hurricanes (WHL)**

The pairing of defence partners can be a real challenge for a coach, especially in the NHL, where the back line is critical to a team's success. Hours of strategic time can be spent thinking about which players are right together: will they mesh, will they compliment each other and will they survive. The Chicago Blackhawks have a dynamic duo with Brent Seabrook and Duncan Keith. During the regular season and in the Blackhawks 2008-09 run for the cup, this pair held their own, with Seabrook coming on strong and proving that he is indeed one of the top defencemen in the NHL.

The Hockey Canada management staff can visualize these two as a winning combination for Team Canada. Both of these players came to the camp with different strengths. What they like about Seabrook is his ability to use his stick effectively. He pokes, prods and defends the puck well against the opposition. Usually, he is the one in the battle against the boards who comes up with the puck, and he can really knock guys off the puck, giving his team the opportunity to clear the zone. This past season (especially in the second half) Seabrook proved that he was also quite capable of playing strong on the power play. This is another great strength and one that has not gone unnoticed by Hockey Canada.

Seabrook is a player who, in minor hockey, was always good. He went in the first round in the bantam draft in 2000 to the Lethbridge Hurricanes and, just a year later at the young age of 16, easily stepped into his defence role for them. It was no surprise that he was drafted fourteenth overall to the Chicago Blackhawks in 2003. He is big, (6'3", 220 lbs), strong, tough, and a good defender. Scouts loved him.

Image provided by Gerry Johansson

Brent Seabrook played in the 1995 Brick Tournament at the age of 10. He spent most of his minor hockey days in South Delta, B.C.

Hockey Hero:
Chris Pronger

Favourite movie:
Men of Honour

Favourite TV show:
Family Guy

Favourite activities outside of hockey:
camping, movies

Person who had most influence on hockey career growing up:
Dad

Favourite singer:
Keith Urban

Most memorable minor hockey experience:
playing for Pacific Vipers in summer hockey

Favourite team growing up:
Vancouver Canucks

Chicago Blackhawks

Brent Seabrook

2009 August orientation camp

Right from the Major Juniors, at the end of his fourth and final year with Lethbridge, he made the big leap to the pros and finished his spring off with the Norfolk Admirals, the Blackhawks AHL affiliate. He played in the last three games of their regular season and then six post-season games. For Seabrook, this stint in the minors was short lived and lasted just one spring.

In the fall of 2005-06, Seabrook showed up for the Blackhawks training camp and found his way onto their roster. His first year as a rookie was decent; he managed to get 32 points with five of those being goals.

Seabrook is no stranger to Hockey Canada either. He's been in those pressure games, and been able to make the trip home with a few gold medals. Starting early in the Hockey Canada system, Seabrook was an alternate captain for the Under-18 team that won gold in Russia. At that tournament, he was named the top defenceman and was named to the tournament All-Star Team.

The natural progression for Seabrook was to play in the Canadian World Junior Team, which he did for two years straight. In 2004, he played in the IIHF World Junior Championship in Finland and won a silver medal. And in 2005, he was on that amazing Canadian World Junior Team that played in Grand Forks,

North Dakota and won the gold. That team was stacked, (in fact many of the players from that team are on this orientation camp roster), and Seabrook played a strong defensive role for Coach Brent Sutter. That tournament started Canada's winning streak at the IIHF World Junior Championship. They had been in a gold medal drought since 1997.

2009 August orientation camp

Seabrook's experience with Hockey Canada didn't end with Juniors and in 2006, he made the trip to Latvia to play in the Men's World Championships.

Seabrook is a naturally gifted defenceman. His pairing with Duncan Keith gives the Hockey Canada management team a little something extra to look at this fall when they make their final notes.

Camp Highlights

Interestingly enough, for the Red and White game, the management staff did not put Seabrook with his Blackhawk partner Duncan Keith. Instead, they wanted to see how he would work with Dion Phaneuf. When Seabrook first came to the camp, he found out he was rooming with his hockey hero, Chris Pronger. When asked what he said to Pronger when he came in their room he said, "Nothing. I just handed him the remote."

		Statistics– **International**						
Year	Team	Event	GP	G	A	PTS	PIM	Result
		Regional						
2002	PAC	WU17	--	--	--	--	--	Silver
		National						
2002	CAN	SU18	5	1	3	4	29	Gold
2003	CAN	WU18	7	3	3	6	4	Gold
2004	CAN	WJC	6	1	2	3	2	Silver
2005	CAN	WJC	5	0	3	3	0	Gold
2006	CAN	WHC	8	0	0	0	2	4th
	CAN	INTL TOTAL	31	5	11	16	37	
	CAN	SR TOTAL	8	0	0	0	2	

MARC STAAL

DEFENCE #18

Shoots: **Left**
Height: **6'4"**
Weight: **202 lbs**
Birthdate: **January 13, 1987**
Birthplace: **Thunder Bay, Ont.**
Hometown: **Thunder Bay, Ont.**
Team: **New York Rangers (NHL)**
MHA: **Thunder Bay MHA**
NHL Draft: **New York Rangers: 2005 (1, 12)**
Last Amateur Club: **Sudbury Wolves (OHL)**

Middle brother of the three Staal boys selected for the 2010 Hockey Canada orientation camp roster, Marc Staal is the only defenceman of the trio. Although he's not the youngest brother, Marc is still considered as young to be invited to the orientation camp, especially as a defenceman. Generally speaking, defencemen take a little longer to develop and mature as players because of the nature of their position. Only a select few young defencemen were chosen for the roster.

This young defenceman earned his way onto the list by having a strong 2008-09 season with the New York Rangers. He played extremely well in the Rangers' first playoff round against the Washington Capitals. The management team was happy with his performance. When scouting, the Hockey Canada management staff noticed that every time Marc was put on the ice against a good player, he held his own. He matched up and didn't back down. He didn't lose control, nor did he flounder under the pressure. He's a strong skater, with a strong body, and has embraced the shut-down role with energy and enthusiasm. The team really likes this about Marc Staal.

Often when matched up against top players, Marc controlled the play. In critical situations in the defensive zone, he doesn't panic, and instead, takes his time with the puck, making sure he makes the right play. Marc is not a player who throws away the puck; he's steady and uses his time effectively.

All the Staal brothers are good hockey players. Although Marc went high in the 2005 NHL Entry Draft (twelfth overall), many questioned his skills and his ability to be an NHLer. Some said that he would be the number one or two defenceman on the blue line,

Image provided by his mother, Linda Staal

Marc Staal played most of his minor hockey with the Thunder Bay Minor Hockey Association. Here he is just starting off.

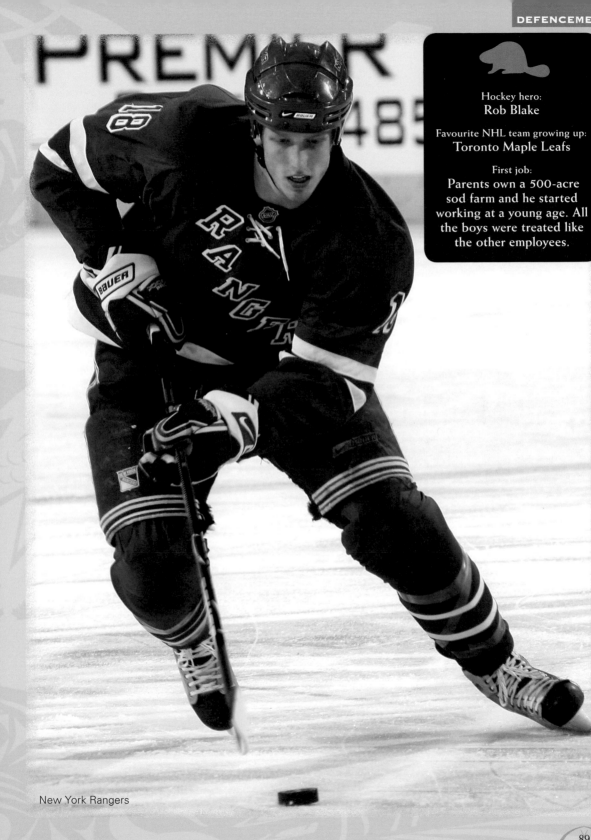

Hockey hero:
Rob Blake

Favourite NHL team growing up:
Toronto Maple Leafs

First job:
Parents own a 500-acre sod farm and he started working at a young age. All the boys were treated like the other employees.

New York Rangers

Marc Staal

while other scouts were shaking their heads in confusion and slotting him as a fifth or sixth man. The mixed opinions and question marks beside Marc's name didn't make a ton of sense, because Marc finished his Junior career with the Sudbury Wolves on a high, winning the Max Kaminsky Trophy as the OHL's Most Outstanding Defenceman for the 2006-07 season. He was also the captain of that team.

In the spring of 2007, Marc also won the Wayne Gretzky 99 Award, as the league's post season MVP. There was no reason for Marc to listen to the media talk about how he might not become a great NHL player. So, he didn't.

Marc showed that he could be that player who just went out and played his game. And sometimes, that game was great. Not everyone in Canada, as a junior, gets the chance to play for the Canadian World Junior Team. It's not an easy invite. Marc earned the right to play on the famous and prestigious Canadian World Junior Team in both 2006 and 2007 at the IIHF World Junior Championships. Both years he came home to Canada wearing a gold medal.

In 2006, after lining up to accept his gold medal, he was named the tournament's top defenceman. That year Marc was paired with defence partner Ryan Parent, and the duo creatively managed to shut down Russian superstar, Evgeni Malkin. This success encouraged the Marc Staal naysayers to revise what they were saying about his NHL career.

Marc is the stay-at-home guy, the defenceman who perhaps doesn't reach the top on all the fan polls. In 2007, on a hockey website, there was a poll taken about which Staal brother would have the best NHL career. The poll answers were Jordan—37 per cent, Eric—25 per cent, Jared—25 per cent and Marc—13 per cent.

Marc has gone on to play a good solid defensive game which captured the attention of the Hockey Canada scouts in his 2008-09 season. He is a player that is capable of defending against the biggest names in the game. This quality alone makes Marc an attractive candidate for 2010, and, if he continues to battle against the biggest and the best in the NHL during the fall of 2009, he very well could have that spot on the 2010 Canadian Olympic Team.

Camp Highlights
Young Marc Staal was paired with Francois Beauchemin, who is not a veteran, but he is still seven years older than Marc. They played well together and Marc moved the puck and made some good passes.

2009 August orientation camp

2009 August orientation camp

Statistics– **International**

Year	Team	Event	GP	G	A	PTS	PIM	Result
				Regional				
2004	ON	WU17	6	0	1	1	2	Gold
				National				
2004	CAN	SU18	5	0	0	0	2	Gold
2006	CAN	WJC	6	0	1	1	4	Gold
2007	CAN	WJC	6	0	0	0	4	Gold
	CAN	INTL TOTAL	17	0	1	1	10	
	CAN	SR TOTAL	0	0	0	0	0	

Marc Staal

SHEA WEBER

DEFENCE #6

Shoots: **Right**
Height: **6'4"**
Weight: **230 lbs**
Birthdate: **August 14, 1985**
Birthplace: **Salmon Arm, B.C.**
Hometown: **Sicamous, B.C.**
Team: **Nashville Predators (NHL)**
MHA: **Sicamous MHA**
NHL Draft: **Nashville Predators: 2003 (2, 49)**
Last Amateur Club: **Kelowna Rockets (WHL)**

The hardest shot from any player on the Hockey Canada roster comes from defenceman, Shea Weber. Not only is his shot hard, but it's accurate, and his one-timers are like rapid-fire bullets. The Hockey Canada management team says Shea Weber "plays with an edge." This doesn't mean that he's always out on the ice looking for a fight, but rather that Weber is a true physical player, who grits his teeth and doesn't back down from anyone, especially when he's in the middle, stirring it up. A big guy (6'4", 230 lbs), he makes his opposition pay the price when they run up against him.

In the past few seasons, Shea Weber has emerged as a solid player who is dependable on the power play. This is a good quality to have, because Hockey Canada needs strong power play players, especially a few who can play on the first power play. Weber is considered a "few years" ahead of some of the other defencemen.

Weber has played his entire NHL career with the Nashville Predators and is known as their top defenceman. According to some media reports, his breakout year was just this past year, but honestly, Shea Weber has been breaking out since he was playing Major Junior for the Kelowna Rockets, starting with them in 2002. In 2004, at the age of 19, he was named to the WHL West Second All-Star Team and to the CHL Memorial Cup All-Star Team. That was the year the Rockets won the Memorial Cup. For three years running, when Weber played for the Rockets, they made it to the Memorial Cup Finals. In 2005, Weber picked up the WHL Air BC Trophy and was named to the WHL West First All-Star Team.

Image provided by Bruce Hamilton from the Kelowna Rockets

Shea Weber played for the Kelowna Rockets in the WHL when they won the Memorial Cup.

Favourite movie:
Slapshot

Idol:
Dad

Favourite activity outside of hockey:
wakesurfing

If not a hockey player would be a:
firefighter

Person who had most influence on hockey career growing up:
Dad

Hockey hero:
Wayne Gretzky

Favourite teams growing up:
Montreal, San Jose, Philadelphia

Favourite book:
Bill Belichick books

2009 August orientation camp

Shea Weber

Halfway through his four-year stint with the Kelowna Rockets, Weber was picked up by the Nashville Predators in the second round, going thirty-ninth overall in the 2003 NHL Entry Draft. Weber made his debut in the NHL on January 6, 2006. He had played his fall season with the Milwaukee Admirals and played well enough in that first game, in early January, to give him a seat on the bench for the rest of Nashville's season. He played 28 games with them. His finish was good for a rookie, and he ended with two goals and ten assists. In the playoff round, Nashville was eliminated in the first round by the San Jose Sharks but Weber managed to pick up two playoff goals.

Immediately following Nashville's elimination, Weber headed back to the minors and played a significant role in the Admirals run for the Calder Cup. Unfortunately, the Admirals lost in six games to the Hershey Bears.

In the 2006-07 season, Weber became one of Nashville's most important defenceman but in 2007-08 he suffered numerous injuries and could only play 54 games. This could be the reason why many have said that his breakout season was in 2008–09. Healthy, he came to Nashville's line in the fall of 2008 and totally dominated his position, making many stand up and take notice of his skills as a defenceman.

A Hockey Canada veteran, Weber has two gold medals and one silver medal to his credit. In 2005 in North Dakota, he played on Canada's World Junior Team, winning the gold medal. Then, in 2007, he made the big hurdle and played in the 2007 IIHF Men's World Championship, winning another gold medal. And just last spring, Weber played in the IIHF Men's World Championship, winning a silver medal, and being named top defenceman by the IIHF Directorate.

Everything he has earned to date, his trophies and awards, have certainly helped make Shea Weber a solid contender for this 2010 Olympic Team.

But really, it is his physical play and his edge that puts him in the front running. If he continues breaking out this fall—or in perhaps simpler terms, just keeps playing the way he has always played—his name could very well be on the final roster.

Nashville Predators

2009 August orientation camp

Camp Highlights

Shea Weber used his puck moving strengths, determination and shooting to compliment Scott Niedermayer's finesse and brains. Together they were a great defence tandem.

Year	Team	Event	GP	G	A	PTS	PIM	Result
Statistics– **International**								
		Regional						
		Not applicable						
		National						
2005	CAN	WJC	6	1	1	2	31	Gold
2007	CAN	WHC	6	0	0	0	10	Gold
2009	CAN	WHC	9	4	8	12	6	Silver
	CAN	INTL TOTAL	21	5	9	14	47	
	CAN	SR TOTAL	15	4	8	12	16	

Shea Weber

JEFF CARTER

FORWARD #17

Shoots: **Right**
Height: **6'3"**
Weight: **200 lbs**
Birthdate: **January 1, 1985**
Birthplace: **London, Ont.**
Hometown: **London, Ont.**
Team: **Philadelphia Flyers (NHL)**
MHA: **Elgin-Middlesex MHA**
NHL Draft: **Philadelphia Flyers: 2003 (1, 11)**
Last Amateur Club: **Sault Ste. Marie Greyhounds (OHL)**

Since the day he started playing in the NHL, Jeff Carter has been a goal scorer. With great breakout speed, and a great shot—two lethal combinations for a forward—he is a definite offensive threat. These attributes, and his amazing international statistics, were good enough for Hockey Canada to invite him to the orientation camp.

In back to back years, Carter played for Canada in the World Junior Championships. His first trip to the IIHF World Junior Championships was in 2004, when he went to Finland with the team and returned home with a silver medal. Then in 2005, he was an alternate captain for the prestigious team that won a gold medal in North Dakota, and because there are so many players on this roster from that team, there is some built-in chemistry. Each year he played in the World Junior Championship, Carter was named to the World Junior All-Star Team.

In those two years with Hockey Canada, he scored 12 goals, which placed him in a tie with Eric Lindros as all-time goal scoring leader at the World Junior Championship. A note must be made that while Carter is tied with Lindros, Lindros played in an additional tournament than Jeff. Carter also played for Canada at the 2003 IIHF Under-18 Championship in Russia where he scored six goals in seven games. Those stats prove that Carter was a scoring threat at a young age.

This scoring ability was also evident when he played Major Junior for the Sault Ste. Marie Greyhounds. Every year he accumulated points, even in his first year, at just 16 years old, he managed to scavenge 18 goals and 17 assists. As he matured and

Jeff Carter grew up in London, Ontario, playing most of his minor hockey career in Elgin-Middlesex MHA.

Image provided by his mother, Sue Carter

2009 August orientation camp

Favourite TV show:
Two and a Half Men

Hockey Hero:
Doug Gilmour

Favourite activity outside of hockey:
boating

If not a hockey player would be an:
architect

Person who had most influence on
hockey career growing up:
Dad

Favourite minor hockey coach:
Dad

Best concert ever attended:
Pearl Jam

Favourite team growing up:
Toronto Maple Leafs

Favourite magazine:
Us

Jeff Carter

CANADA

continued to play for the Greyhounds, Carter's scoring improved. In the 2002-03 season, at 17, he had 35 goals and 36 assists for 71 points. That spring in the 2003 Entry Draft, Carter went in the first round, eleventh overall to the Philadelphia Flyers.

He played for the Greyhounds for four years, recording his career high in the 2004-05 season when he managed 74 points (34 goals, 40 assists).

This high earned him a spot on the First Team OHL All-Star Team as well as the OHL and CHL Sportsman of the year award. In 2005, when the Greyhounds finished their season, Carter accepted the call-up to play with the Flyers American Hockey League affiliate, the Philadelphia Phantom. As luck would have it, this team made it to the finals and ended up winning the Calder Cup. Carter played 21 playoff games and recorded a fantastic 23 points (12 goals, 11 assists). He was also the MVP of the Calder Cup.

This young hockey player didn't slow down when he made his debut into the NHL, and he scored his first career goal early in the season, on October 24 against Roberto Luongo of the Florida Panthers.

Carter has produced, for three years now with the Philadelphia Flyers. But his best season was his last, 2008-09, when he beat his own record by scoring 46 goals and garnering 38 assists for a total of 84 points. It was this scoring action that got the Hockey Canada scouts buzzing.

The Hockey Canada management team hasn't talked much about this young man's defensive skills, after all he was chosen for the camp as a goal-scorer and a tremendous skater. Past stats from Hockey Canada Teams and the NHL will hold well in his favour but he will have to produce some goals in the start of the 2009-10 to survive, and find a spot on the final roster.

2009 August orientation camp

Camp Highlights

Carter started off playing wing on a line with Brendan Morrow and Michael Richards, and true to form, he put the puck in the net. In the second period he scored the first goal for Team Red at 6:17 to even up the score and make it 1-1.

Home Ice

Philadelphia Flyers

Year	Team	Event	GP	G	A	PTS	PIM	Result
Statistics– **International**								
Regional								
2002	ONT	WU17	6	5	3	8	4	Bronze
National								
2003	CAN	WU18	7	2	4	6	2	Gold
2004	CAN	WJC	6	5	2	7	2	Silver
2005	CAN	WJC	6	7	3	10	6	Gold
2006	CAN	WHC	9	4	2	6	2	4th
	CAN	INTL TOTAL	28	18	11	29	12	
	CAN	SR TOTAL	9	4	2	6	2	

DAN CLEARY

FORWARD #11

Shoots: **Left**
Height: **6'0"**
Weight: **210 lbs**
Birthdate: **December 18, 1978**
Birthplace: **Carbonear, Nfld**
Hometown: **Harbour Grace, Nfld**
Team: **Detroit Red Wings (NHL)**
MHA: **Tri Pen Frost MHA**
NHL Draft: **Chicago Blackhawks: 1993 (1, 7)**
Last Amateur Club: **Oshawa Generals (OHL)**

CANADA

Sometimes life is ironic. Cut from the Canadian World Junior Team three times, Dan Cleary found himself on Team Canada's 2010 Olympic orientation-camp roster. Team Canada Executive Director, Steve Yzerman, made a statement about the selection process and said, "We wanted to bring some different types of players, some guys that maybe aren't leading their teams in scoring but are very good players in a different role."

This kind of selection process is great for a player like Dan Cleary because he can play so many positions and in each one he finds success. When he received the news of his orientation camp invite, he was ecstatic. He had been on the golf course with his cell phone off and when he turned it on and received the message telling him he'd been invited to the camp, he simply couldn't believe it. Cleary was the only Detroit Red Wing invited to the camp.

Born in 1978, Cleary is part of the "older generation" of players, those who have been around the NHL for quite some time. He's been at this game for a while, and has continued to work to perfect his own game.

So what was it about Cleary that the Hockey Canada management team liked? He's not a huge goal scorer, nor is he key on the power play.

Cleary is the guy who can play a number of positions on the bench. In any situation, he plays great. He can move up the bench and be part of the top six grouping or he can move down the bench and be the fourth-line guy. When called upon to play the fourth line, he immediately jumps to the energy roll. Hockey Canada needs those kinds of players, guys who are smart and who don't

Dan Cleary grew up in Newfoundland. This photo was taken when he was at a summer hockey camp.

Idol:
Tiger Woods

Favourite movie:
Braveheart

Pre-competetion rituals:
**watching TV, having tea
with my girls**

Most memorable
minor hockey experience:
winning the Hostess Cup

Hockey hero:
Gary Roberts

Favourite team growing up:
Calgary Flames

Favourite magazine:
Golf Digest

Favourite book:
**Tuesdays with Morrie
by Mitch Albom**

2009 August orientation camp

Dan Cleary

mind playing less minutes in a game for the greater good of the team. They move, they shuffle, they do their job and they do it well. Cleary can move up and down the bench, without hesitation, without blinking, without saying a word.

Cleary is also on this roster because he has really emerged as a strong two-way player. Often, he goes to places that a lot of other players won't go to, such as the deep corners. Plus, Steve Yzerman knows him well, and likes how he plays.

As a young teen, Cleary was a superstar. In his first game with the Belleville Bulls at the age of 16 he scored a hat trick. The next year he registered a whooping 115 points, having collected 53 goals and 62 assists. And then a shift occurred for Cleary in the next year and he began a steady downward decline. The next year his points total went down to 80 (32 goals, 48 assists), and the following year, in 1996–97 which was his draft year, he only managed 47 points, although he did only play 30 games for the Bulls that year.

Despite the dramatic change in his points he was still drafted thirteenth overall by the Chicago Blackhawks. He put in time with the AHL and the NHL, going up and down like a yo-yo until he was traded to the Edmonton Oilers in 1999. Four years later, he was again on the chopping block and was signed for a cheaper contract to the Phoenix Coyotes. When the lockout was over, Cleary was not given a qualifying contract with the Coyotes and was invited to the Detroit Red Wings camp.

Detroit Red Wings

With the Red Wings, Cleary brought back some of the stardom he'd seen as a 16-year-old, especially in 2006-07 when he scored a NHL career high of 20 goals.

It was during the run to the Stanley Cup in 2007-08, that Cleary proved he was a player to be reckoned with. Over the years, to keep himself in the game, he had made a conscious effort to become more than the goal scorer that he had been when he was young and playing Junior Hockey. To survive in the NHL, he had to learn how to be a defensive forward, to play the two-way game, which he has done successfully.

As far as international experience, Cleary has only played in one Men's World Championship in 2002. The team put in a drastic performance because it was so soon after the 2002 Olympic gold medal victory that many players decided not to play for Canada.

So how will a player like Dan Cleary fare when the finale unfolds? It depends on how the Hockey Canada management team rolls the dice when the final roster is being made. If they need a player like Cleary, a guy who can play up and down the lineup, the answer will be easy for them to make.

2009 August orientation camp

Camp Highlights

For the Red and White game, Dan Cleary started off playing wing on a line with Milan Lucic and Andy McDonald. All three players on this line showed their strengths, and Cleary proved he was a good two-way player.

Statistics– **International**								
Year	Team	Event	GP	G	A	PTS	PIM	Result
			Regional					
1994	ATL	WU17						
1995	NL	CWG			unavailable			7th
			National					
1995	CAN	SU18	5	4	4	8	6	Silver
2002	CAN	WHC	7	2	1	3	2	6th
	CAN	INTL TOTAL	7	2	1	3	2	
	CAN	SR TOTAL	7	2	1	3	2	

SIDNEY CROSBY

FORWARD #87

Shoots: **Left**
Height: **5'11"**
Weight: **200 lbs**
Birthdate: **August 7, 1987**
Birthplace: **Halifax, N.S.**
Hometown: **Cole Harbour, N.S.**
Team: **Pittsburgh Penguins (NHL)**
MHA : **Cole Harbour MHA**
NHL Draft: **Pittsburgh Penguins: 2005 (1, 1)**
Last Amateur Club: **Océanic de Rimouski (QMJHL)**

After Sidney Crosby won the Crosby/Ovechkin showdown during the 2009 NHL playoffs and captained his Pittsburgh Penguins to the Stanley Cup finals for the second straight year, Steve Yzerman recognized that Crosby had earned a top spot on his 2010 Olympic Team.

Many questioned the decisions that left Crosby off the 2006 Olympic team. The first camp for that team was held in August 2005, before Sidney made his professional debut, though even after he proved himself that fall by starting off his NHL career with one monstrous bang, when the final roster was announced for the Olympic Team in December of 2005, Crosby's name was not there.

Four years later, while Crosby is still relatively young, he plays at the professional level with tremendous confidence and experience. He is a fierce competitor and the youngest player ever to captain his team to a Stanley Cup Championship. Crosby is talented, skilled, and has wisdom well beyond his years. The Hockey Canada management team classifies him as "being close to the perfect player." He took his Penguins team to the Stanley Cup finals by playing gritty, determined, and highly skilled mature hockey.

Crosby began playing international hockey for Hockey Canada at the early age of 16. He had turned 16 on August 7, and by Christmas of the same year had been named to the official roster of the IIHF World Junior Team that competed in the 2004 World Junior Championships in Helsinki, Finland. Only four other players had ever made a World Junior team at 16: Jay Bouwmeester, Jason Spezza, Eric Lindros, and Wayne Gretzky. In Canada's game against Switzerland, Crosby became the youngest player to score a goal at the IIHF World

Image provided by his mother, Trina Crosby

Big smile for Sidney Crosby, who has always loved playing hockey. This photo was taken in 2000 when he was playing Peewee AAA.

Idol:
Michael Jordan

Favourite movie:
The Replacements

Favourite activity outside of hockey:
fishing

If not a hockey player would be a:
fireman or policeman

Person who had most influence on
hockey career growing up:
Mom and Dad

Favourite band:
Great Big Sea

Hockey hero:
Steve Yzerman

Favourite team growing up:
Montreal Canadiens

2009 August orientation camp

Sidney Crosby

Junior Championships, helping his team win 7-2. That year, the team picked up a silver medal and Crosby finished the tournament with 2 goals and 3 assists in six games. Sidney is a natural motivator and while his points helped his team on the ice, so too did his presence both on the bench and in the dressing room where he worked well with teammates and coaching staff and was a source of encouragement. Not bad for being just 16 years, 5 months and 21 days old.

When it came time to pick the team the following year, Crosby's name was right up there again. The 2005 IIHF World Championships were played in Grand Forks North Dakota that year and Canada won the gold medal by annihilating Russia 6-1. Crosby improved his personal results from the prior year and picked up six goals and three assists in the tournament.

Although Crosby was eligible to play in three more World Juniors after the Grand Forks tournament, that 2005 team would be his last Junior appearance. Sidney was ranked number one going into the 2005 NHL Entry Draft and, as expected, was picked number one in the first round by the Pittsburgh Penguins. He was put into their lineup immediately. Sidney's NHL debut was nothing short of incredible and he quickly earned a key role with the Penguins. As one of their top players, Pittsburgh could not afford to lose him from the lineup and give him time off from the team to play in the World Juniors. He finished his rookie season in the NHL, at the age of 18, with 39 goals and 63 assists for 102 points.

Crosby has had one other opportunity to play with Team Canada and that was in 2006 when he competed in the IIHF World Championships in Latvia. Named as the alternate captain, Sidney registered eight goals and eight assists in nine games and made yet one more record happen by being the youngest player ever to win a World Championship scoring title. The Canadian team finished in the non-medal fourth place but Crosby was named as the tournament's top forward and to the All-Star Team.

Crosby has grown into a mighty mature package both on and off the ice. He is almost a perfect player and a true role model for young children across Canada that aspire to represent this nation at the international level and live their dream playing in the NHL. Sidney's hockey prowess is complemented by his amazing character and the fact that he is genuinely a sincere and respectable man. Sidney is liked for the numbers

Pittsburgh Penguins

CANADA

he puts on the scoreboard, though he is also liked because of who he is. Canada is fortunate having such an ambassador for our nation and our sport.

Camp Highlights

Sidney Crosby and Rick Nash looked darn good together. In the Red and White game they started off with Jarome Iginla but then Coach Babcock changed things up and put Martin St. Louis on the line. This line seemed to click.

The day before the camp, Sidney was worried as he was still in Nova Scotia and Hurricane Bill was heading toward the East Coast. He was so concerned about not getting out of Nova Scotia because of plane delays that he phoned Hockey Canada. He did not want to miss the first ice session. Hockey Canada worked with the Sport Minister of Canada to get him on an earlier flight even though the planes were quite full because of the impeding weather condition. But Sidney was insistent; he didn't want to be late. That's called commitment.

2009 August orientation camp

Statistics– International								
Year	Team	Event	GP	G	A	PTS	PIM	Result
Regional								
2003	NS	CWG	5	9	7	16	16	6th
National								
2003	CAN	SU18	5	4	2	6	10	4th
2004	CAN	WJC	5	2	3	5	10	Silver
2005	CAN	WJC	6	6	3	9	4	Gold
2006	CAN	WHC	9	8	8	16	10	4th
	CAN	INTL TOTAL	25	20	16	36	34	
	CAN	SR TOTAL	9	8	8	16	10	

SHANE DOAN

FORWARD #19

Shoots: **Right**
Height: **6'3"**
Weight: **216 lbs**
Birthdate: **October 10, 1976**
Birthplace: **Eston, Saskatchewan**
Hometown: **Halkirk, Alta.**
Team: **Phoenix Coyotes (NHL)**
MHA: **Castor MHA**
NHL Draft: **Winnipeg Jets: 1995 (1, 7)**
Last Amateur Club: **Kamloops Blazers (WHL)**

A true Hockey Canada veteran, Shane Doan has definitely earned his spot on this orientation-camp roster. He has committed a great deal of his time to Hockey Canada over the years, and has often assumed the role as team captain.

Having played eight times for Team Canada, Doan is a permanent fixture. He started his Hockey Canada career in 1999 when he played for Canada at the IIHF World Championship. His last stint was at the 2009 IIHF World Championships in Switzerland. In between he played in the World Championships in 2004, 2005, 2007, 2008. He also played in the 2006 Winter Olympics and in the 2004 World Cup of Hockey. In total he has earned an incredible collection of hardware, including two gold medals, one World Cup, and three silver medals.

Of course, the question is being asked (as it is being asked of all players on this roster): Will Shane Doan be announced as a finalist? Will his past be enough to determine his future?

Let's strip Doan of his international experience and see what he has left to offer this team. According to the Hockey Canada management team, Doan is valued because he can play in any situation, and has demonstrated this ability consistently throughout his career, particularly in international competition. Doan is also one of those players, like Cleary, that can play up and down the lineup. Put him in with the top six forwards and he'll certainly do his job and blend in with the line. And while he may not necessarily end up with the most goals, he will definitely assist his linemates and help the puck find the net. Doan works tirelessly to win.

Image provided by Sergey Kocharo from the Phoenix Coyotes

Here Shane Doan is doing a victory cheer, while he played Major Junior for the Kamloops Blazers in the WHL.

Hockey heroes:
Paul Coffey, Bobby Orr

Favourite minor hockey coach:
Bernie Doan

Favourite TV show:
House

If not a hockey player
would be a:
**someone who works
with horses.**

Best concert ever attended:
U2, Garth Brooks

Pre-game meal:
Eggs

Favourite song on mp3 player:
**Montgomery Gentry:
Roll with Me**

Favourite book:
**The Shack by
WM. Paul Young**

2009 August orientation camp

Shane Doan

When playing at his peak, he can score as well as any other player in the league. Alternatively, if moved down to the fourth line, Doan will rally and be that energy player needed to fill that vital spot. Doan makes the most of his time on the ice, and can achieve great things on a 30-second shift. The Hockey Canada management team also see Doan as one of those players that will benefit from the smaller ice surface they'll meet in Vancouver.

It must also be noted that Doan is a leader, and even if he's not named as captain, he'll subtlety provide his leadership experience without stepping on the toes of those who have been designated captains. Doan has captained Canada at the IIHF World Championships three consecutive years in a row, and he has been the captain of the Phoenix Coyotes since 2003.

As a player, Doan handles leadership with dignity. He has met controversy during his career and it is how Doan responds to adversity that documents his character and his ability to remain focused on the ice, even following a conflict. Prior to the 2007 IIHF Men's World Championships in Russia, Doan was made a political victim because of something he was alleged to have said on the ice to a French Official. A parliamentary politician wanted the 'C' taken off his jersey. Hockey Canada defended Doan, supporting him 100 per cent. The best thing about the entire fiasco was Doan's retribution. In his first IIHF World Championship game in 2007, just after the incident, Doan stepped on the ice and scored a hat trick.

Doan's career began like most in the Major Juniors, where he was a star. In 1995, his team, the Kamloops Blazers won the Memorial Cup, and Doan won the Stafford Smythe Memorial Trophy as tournament MVP. That spring, he was drafted by the Winnipeg Jets in the first round, seventh overall. On a historical note, Doan was the final first-round pick for the Jets before the franchise moved to Phoenix.

A loyal player, Doan is moving into his thirteenth year with the Phoenix Coyotes. As for his name being on the final roster, a lot will depend on what this thirteenth season holds for him. Maybe 13 will be his lucky year.

Camp Highlights

Shane Doan is a natural leader and this was apparent at the camp. He is good with the young guys and makes everyone feel as if they are part of the team. The Red and White game wasn't Shane's type of game because he is a hard hitter, but the management team knows this and will watch him in the fall.

2009 August
orientation camp

Phoenix Coyotes

Statistics– International								
Year	Team	Event	GP	G	A	PTS	PIM	Result
			Regional					
			Not applicable					
			National					
1999	CAN	WHC	4	0	0	0	0	4th
2003	CAN	WHC	9	4	2	6	12	Gold
2004	CAN	WC	6	1	1	2	4	1st
2005	CAN	WHC	9	1	3	4	2	Silver
2006	CAN	OLY	6	2	1	3	2	7th
2007	CAN	WHC	9	5	5	10	8	Gold
2008	CAN	WHC	9	2	4	6	6	Silver
2009	CAN	WHC	9	1	6	7	14	Silver
	CAN	INTL TOTAL	61	16	22	38	48	
	CAN	SR TOTAL	61	16	22	38	48	

Shane Doan

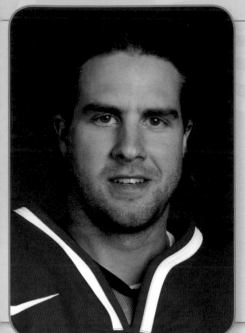

SIMON GAGNE

FORWARD #12

Shoots: **Left**
Height: **6'0"**
Weight: **195 lbs**
Birthdate: **February 29, 1980**
Birthplace: **Quebec City, QC**
Hometown: **Ste-Foy, QC**
Team: **Philadelphia Flyers (NHL)**
MHA: **AHM de Ste-Foy**
NHL Draft: **Philadelphia Flyers: 1998 (1, 22)**
Last Amateur Club: **Remparts de Québec (QMJHL)**

Some hockey players are true offensive scorers, some are considered grinders, and others are what the Hockey Canada management team have classified as "complete" players. Simon Gagne is in the latter category. Stats alone indicate that he can put the puck in the net, but he also plays a strong, structural defensive game. Beside his name in the management binder is the phrase, "plays both ends of the rink." He is also a "good complement" player. This Olympic squad will need some players like Gagne to round out the lines. They need that guy who can do the job no matter what.

Gagne is another veteran player who has international Hockey Canada experience dating back a number of years. Like Doan, he started his Hockey Canada career in 1999 at the IIHF World Junior Championships in Winnipeg, winning his first silver medal. On top of his game, Gagne scored seven goals in the tournament and tied a team record by scoring four goals in one game. The person he tied with was the legendary Mario Lemieux who had accomplished the same feat 16 years earlier at the 1983 World Junior Championships.

Over the years, Gagne has answered the call to play in four other Hockey Canada tournaments, winning one gold medal, one World Cup title, and one more silver medal. He picked up his gold medal when he played for the famous 2002 Olympic team, (where he was the youngest player on the team), and in 2004 he picked up his World Cup when he played for the prestigious World Cup of Hockey team. Both of those teams were true winning teams, and that helps the selection process. The Hockey Canada management team likes proven winners.

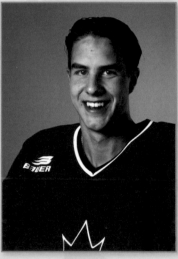

Image provided by Hockey Canada

This is Simon Gagne's head shot when he played for the 1999 IIHF World Junior Championship Team in Winnipeg, helping Canada to win the silver medal.

Nickname:
Gags

Spends off seasons in:
Ste-Foy Quebec

Something you might
not know about Simon:
he is the only active NHL
player and one of only five
in league history to be born
on February 29

Organizations/Charities
supported:
annual golf tournament
supports Leukemia
research, also sponsors
amateur athlete Catherine
Roberge (judo).

Favourite activities
outside of hockey:
movies, golf

Hockey hero:
Joe Sakic, Michael Goulet

Favourite NHL team growing up:
Quebec Nordiques

2009 August orientation camp

Simon Gagne

The second silver medal put around Gagne's neck came in 2005, when he played in the IIHF Men's World Championship. Four years after the incredible 2002 Olympic victory, Gagne also made the 2006 Olympic team. And of course, further explanation of that team is not important.

Over his long career, Gagne has earned many awards. He started off as a 16-year-old in the QMJHL playing for the Beuport Harfangs, where he played mostly on the third and fourth lines.

Steadily, he climbed the ladder of success, and in 1998, he was drafted twenty-second overall by the Philadelphia Flyers. At the end of his 1998-99 season, now playing with the Quebec Remparts, he had collected an amazing 120 points (50 goals, 70 assists), and a plus/minus of +51. He finished sixth in the league in scoring, was awarded to the QMJHL Second All-Star Team and was honoured with the Paul Dumont Trophy as the "personality of the year." In the fall of 1999, the Quebec Remparts retired Gagne's number 12 jersey. Only two players from the Quebec Remparts have had their jerseys retired. Along with Gagne is the more-than-famous Guy Lafleur.

Since his Junior years, Gagne has only played for the Philadelphia Flyers organization. He's had some great years but he's also had some injuries. His best season as a pro was in 2004-05 when he scored 47 goals and totalled

2009 August
orientation camp

114

Home Ice

79 points. This was the year he was on the famous "Deuces Wild" line with Forsberg and Knuble. Possibly his worst season as a pro was in 2007-08, when he suffered a possible three concussions in five months. The first concussion happened in October, the second in November and the third in February. The doctors sidelined Gagne and he didn't play a game past February 20.

With that in mind, the Hockey Canada scouts watched Gagne carefully in the 2008-09 season, and were happy when he came out strong, scoring 34 goals for 74 points with a +21 average. He also managed to play 74 games.

Gagne is a veteran, a two-way "complete" player. Let's hope he has a strong and healthy opening to the 2009-10 season.

Camp Highlights
Unfortunately, Simon Gagne suffered an injury at camp and was only on the ice for the first ice session. He will be looked at in the fall of 2009.

August orientation camp

Statistics– **International**								
Year	Team	Event	GP	G	A	PTS	PIM	Result
Regional								
Not applicable								
National								
1997	CAN	SU18	7	3	1	4	0	Gold
1999	CAN	WJC	7	7	1	8	2	Silver
2002	CAN	OLY	6	7	3	10	6	Gold
2004	CAN	WC	6	1	1	2	0	1st
2005	CAN	WHC	9	3	7	10	0	Silver
2006	CAN	OLY	6	1	2	3	0	7th
	CAN	INTL TOTAL	41	22	15	37	8	
	CAN	SR TOTAL	27	6	11	17	6	

RYAN GETZLAF

FORWARD #15

Shoots: **Right**
Height: **6′4″**
Weight: **221 lbs**
Birthdate: **May 10, 1985**
Birthplace: **Regina, Sask.**
Hometown: **Regina, Sask.**
Team: **Anaheim Ducks (NHL)**
MHA: **Regina Rangers MHA**
NHL Draft: **Anaheim Mighty Ducks: 2003 (1, 19)**
Last Amateur Club: **Calgary Hitmen (WHL)**

CANADA

What can be said about Getzlaf? He's an elite power forward. He scores, he checks, he fights, he hits—he basically does everything that a hockey player needs to do to get the job done. The Hockey Canada management team likes that he can "control a game physically, but can also score." So, he's not really a specialist, but an all-around good player. Plus, let's not forget that his 6′4″, 221 pound frame makes him an intimidating force on the ice, as well as a powerful forward.

He's not really young, but he's not quite a veteran, yet he has experience in big games and he knows international hockey.

In 2007-08, Getzlaf won his first, and only, Stanley Cup when the Anaheim Ducks beat out the Ottawa Senators in six games. During the 2007 playoffs, Getzlaf led his team in scoring with 17 points in 21 games, and was one of their key players in every situation. He was Anaheim's go-to guy who helped them earn the Cup.

In international hockey, Getzlaf won a gold medal when he played on the 2005 World Junior Team in North Dakota. Yes, this was that stacked team, and Getzlaf helped make it that way by scoring a goal and two assists in the final game against Russia, ensuring that Canada take the game 6-1. He also finished the tournament second in scoring with 12 points. His other Hockey Canada medals were both silver from the 2004 IIHF World Junior Championship, and from the 2008 Men's World Championship. In his senior debut in 2008, Getzlaf rallied to score 14 points in just nine games.

Just this past season, 2008-09, Getzlaf ended up tied for sixth in the NHL scoring race for the regular season with 25 goals and

Growing up in Regina, Ryan Getzlaf played minor hockey for the Regina Rangers.

Image provided by Gerry Johannson

Nickname:
Getzy

Sports highlights:
won high school MVP awards for volleyball, baseball, and floor hockey

Other sports highlight:
was a catcher for the Regina White Sox at the 1998 Canadian Peewee Baseball Championship

Organization/Charities supported:
Ronald McDonald House

Favourite activities outside hockey:
wake-boarding and riding Sea-Doos in the summer

The 2005 IIHF World Junior Championship was one of the best Junior teams Canada has ever had.

Ryan Getzlaf

Here is Ryan leaving practice when he played for the 2005 IIHF World Junior Championship Team.

91 points. His sixth place finish was matched in the playoffs when he scored four goals and 18 points in just 13 games. The amount of assists that Getzlaf picks up demonstrates his role as a team player, and shows that he is a guy who passes the puck well and helps to set up goals for his linemates.

Typically, Getzlaf was that good, young player who made Major Junior, but he wasn't the best player. In the bantam draft, he went third round, fifty-fourth overall to the Calgary Hitmen. Not exactly at the top of the heap. The Hitmen took a chance on him anyway, and, in his rookie season, he scored 18 points, nothing to make anyone stand up and take notice. But in his next season with the Hitmen, he improved his stats dramatically, by posting 68 points. That was enough to get him drafted in the first round, nineteenth overall, in the 2003 Entry Draft to the Anaheim Ducks. Getzlaf wasn't the shoe-in guy, who shows up at an NHL training camp after draft year and immediately makes the roster. Putting in parts of two years in the AHL, Getzlaf made his NHL debut in the fall of 2005-06 and from there he has continued to play with the Ducks.

This past summer, Getzlaf underwent surgery to repair a torn abdominal muscle. Although the injury happened late last spring at the end of the season, it didn't stop him from playing in the playoffs. But when he started his training regime early in the summer, the problem persisted and he knew surgery was his only option. This sports-hernia type of surgery is common as five Ducks players have had it done. Recovery times are different for each player.

As far as his status goes for the Hockey Canada orientation camp, Getzlaf was not in the lineup. Team Canada's Executive Director, Steve Yzerman, has talked to Getzlaf and told him that his position on the Olympic team will not be compromised by his lack of on-ice attendance in August.

A true team player, Getzlaf did attend the camp to be a part of the process, bond with the other players, and hopefully to learn the systems that Hockey Canada wants to implement.

The real test, and evaluation for Getzlaf, will be what he accomplishes during the first half of the 2009-10 season with the Anaheim Ducks. But then, the same is true for all of the players on the roster. The season counts for more than the camp.

Camp Highlights
Ryan Getzlaf was in attendance at the camp, showed up for all the events, but didn't play. He did say he would be ready to play at the beginning of the season. The management team looks forward to watching him perform.

Anaheim Ducks

Statistics– **International**								
Year	Team	Event	GP	G	A	PTS	PIM	Result
Regional								
2002	WEST	WU17	5	2	6	8	10	
National								
2003	CAN	WU18	7	2	2	4	10	Gold
2004	CAN	WJC	6	3	3	6	4	Silver
2005	CAN	WJC	6	6	3	9	12	Gold
2008	CAN	WHC	6	3	9	12	8	Silver
	CAN	INTL TOTAL	25	14	17	31	34	
	CAN	SR TOTAL	25	14	17	31	34	

Ryan Getzlaf

DANY HEATLEY

FORWARD #15

Shoots: **Left**
Height: **6'3"**
Weight: **216 lbs**
Birthdate: **January 21, 1981**
Birthplace: **Freiburg, Germany**
Hometown: **Calgary, Alta.**
Team: **San Jose Sharks (NHL)**
MHA: **Hockey Calgary**
NHL Draft: **Atlanta Thrashers: 2000 (1, 2)**
Last Amateur Club: **University of Wisconsin (WCHA)**

CANADA

Dan Heatley's big announcement led to a lot of pressure and media attention. At the end of the 2008-09 season, Heatley made the huge decision to leave the Ottawa Senators. He requested a trade. New coaches had taken over the helm in February, 2009 and for some reason the Senators organization wasn't sitting well with Heatley anymore. His trade demand perked the interest of the Edmonton Oilers, but when they came knocking, Heatley decided to leave the door unanswered.

At the time of the orientation camp, Heatley had not signed with any other NHL team and his agents were still exploring options. Then on September 13th, Dany held a press conference to announce that he had been traded to the San Jose Sharks.

Heatley is a great Hockey Canada supporter, and he knew that his tumultuous summer might cause added media attention at the camp. He knew this was not something that Hockey Canada wanted or needed. Heatley promised Hockey Canada that he would make sure that his issues would not take precedence, so he held his own press conference in Kelowna prior to camp to make sure that his news wasn't the centre of attention. The management team appreciated Heatley's sensitivity, and they only have good things to say about this true-scoring winger. When Heatley is around the net, he needs little opening to score goals. If there is a little hole somewhere, Heatley will use his powerful shot to rifle the puck to the back of the net. Often, the goalie doesn't stand a chance. He's also darn good at creating scoring opportunities for his fellow teammates. But if the truth is told, he will fire the puck first. He loves to score goals.

Image provided by his mother, Karin

Dany Heatley grew up in Calgary, Alberta, and played with the South Four Minor Hockey Association.

2009 August orientation camp

Favourite minor hockey coach:
my dad

Idol:
John Lennon

Favourite movie:
Major League

Favourite activity outside of hockey:
boating

Favourite band:
Dave Matthews Band

Hockey Hero:
Brett Hull

Favourite team growing up:
St. Louis Blues

Favourite book:
**Namath:
A Biography by
Mark Kriegel**

Dany Heatley

CANADA

In the Hockey Canada archives, in their stash of notes, there is a line that says that Heatley is, "Canada's modern-day World Championship leader in goals (38), assists (24) and points (62)." These stats come from the fact that he has played for ten Hockey Canada teams. Yes, he can be considered a true veteran, as well as a true goal scorer.

It would take two pages to list his accomplishments with Hockey Canada teams so let's pinpoint his highlight years. In 2004, he played at the IIHF World Championships in the Czech Republic, and after the Canadian team won the gold medal, Heatley was named the top forward and MVP. Then at the 2008 IIHF World Championships in Quebec City/Halifax, although the team fell short and only won the silver medal, Heatley was named to the All-Star Team and was named the IIHF Directorate's Top Forward and MVP. Heatley holds the Canadian record for most career points at the IIHF World Championship, (52), most career goals (38), most goals in one IIHF World Championship (12), and he also shares the record for most points at one IIHF World Championship (20) with the Executive Director of the Canada's 2010 Olympic Team, Steve Yzerman (1990).

Heatley didn't take the Major Junior route as so many players on this roster did. Instead, Heatley decided to follow in his father's footsteps and play Junior 'A' in the hopes of gaining the attention of some American colleges. Winning the Canadian Junior Player of the Year in 1999, helped his college offers. The decision of where to play wasn't hard for Heatley, because he ended up accepting an offer at his father's alma mater, the University of Wisconsin. His first year, Heatley was voted Rookie of the Year for the WCHA (Western College Hockey Association), won First Team honours, was an NCAA All-American, and his team won the WCHA title.

After one year at college, at the 2000 NHL Entry Draft, Heatley went in the first round, second overall. He decided to not sign with Atlanta, and instead went back to school. It wasn't until the spring that he made his decision to play in the NHL.

2009 August orientation camp

Playing for the Badgers, in that last year that he remained at college, Heatley was named to the NCAA First All-Star Team in 2001 and was a finalist of the Hobey Baker Award as U.S. College Hockey's top player.

Heatley's jump into the NHL was rewarded immediately that first year when he won the Calder Cup as the NHL's rookie of the year.

Team Canada has been good to Heatley and in return he has been good to them. He does have a dream to win an Olympic gold medal. His name was left off the 2002 roster. But let's see what line he is on, who he plays with, how he fares, in the beginning of the 2009 season with a new team. That will be the test for this talented goal-scorer.

San Jose Sharks

Camp Highlights

Heatley was booed when he stepped on the ice but when he dazzled the crowd with a pretty goal in the shootout, the boos were replaced with hearty cheers. He says he's okay with the booing and knows that "they're hockey fans and they have opinions."

Year	Team	Event	GP	G	A	PTS	PIM	Result
		Statistics– **International**						
		Regional						
		Not applicable						
		National						
2000	CAN	WJC	7	2	2	4	4	Bronze
2001	CAN	WJC	7	3	2	5	10	Bronze
2002	CAN	WHC	7	2	2	4	2	6th
2003	CAN	WHC	9	7	3	10	10	Gold
2004	CAN	WHC	9	8	3	11	4	Gold
2004	CAN	WCH	6	0	2	2	2	1st
2005	CAN	WHC	9	3	4	7	16	Silver
2006	CAN	OLY	5	2	1	3	8	7th
2008	CAN	WHC	9	12	8	20	4	Silver
2009	CAN	WHC	9	6	4	10	8	Silver
	CAN	INTL TOTAL	77	45	31	76	68	
	CAN	SR TOTAL	63	40	27	67	54	

Dany Heatley

JAROME IGINLA

FORWARD #12

Shoots: **Right**
Height: **6'1"**
Weight: **203 lbs**
Birthdate: **July 1, 1977**
Birthplace: **Edmonton, Alta.**
Hometown: **St. Albert, Alta.**
Team: **Calgary Flames (NHL)**
MHA: **St. Albert MHA**
NHL Draft: **Dallas Stars: 1995 (1, 11)**
Last Amateur Club: **Kamloops Blazers (WHL)**

When the words power forward are combined with the word leader, there is one player that immediately comes to mind: Jarome Iginla. Or, if you are lucky enough to get that rare empty seat in the Saddledome to watch a Calgary Flames game, you might hear the name pronounced Jaaaaaaarommmmmme Iginla. He wears number 12 and is a Calgary celebrity, a Canadian hero, and a future Hall of Famer. Flames fans love him. Canadians love him.

The hockey gods were kind when they made Iginla. Blessed with a quick release, his rapid shot sometimes blisters the back of the net, making even the great goalies wonder—"What was that? How did that get by me?" It does because Iginla leans all the way into his shot and has an almost perfect technique, putting every ounce of muscle he has into his release.

The guy is built, and even has a tendency to get overly muscular. When the new rules came into effect, Iginla spent a summer trying to ditch some of his muscle by taking yoga and Pilates classes so he could be faster on the ice. The new rules were put into effect to create fewer stoppages and more flow. Passes from behind the defensive blue line to the attacking blue line would be legal. Quicker skaters would benefit from this kind of flow. Additionally, the center line would be ignored for the "two line pass". Plus, there was to be zero tolerance for hooking, holding, and interference which would allow the quicker, smaller players to squeak by. He showed up at the next fall camp slimmer and a lot faster on his skates. Losing the weight didn't alter his rapid release, make him lose power, and if anything it made it quicker.

Image provided by Sean Kelso of the Calgary Flames

Here is a young Jarome Iginla playing centre, and ready to win the faceoff. He played his minor hockey career in St. Albert MHA.

Calgary Flames

Idols:
Tiger Woods, Michael Jordan

Favourite TV show:
Big Brother

Person who had most influence on hockey career growing up:
grandfather (Richard Scheuchard)

If not a hockey player would be a:
lawyer

Favourite band:
Nickelback

Hockey heroes:
Wayne Gretzky, Mark Messier

Favourite team growing up:
Edmonton Oilers

Favourite book:
River God by Wilbur Smith

Jarome Iginla

CANADA

Iginla moves to the net well, makes himself open to receive a pass, or tip in the puck, and is always there to capitalize on a scoring opportunity. He circles and looks for an opening spot where he can fire off his shot with incredible accuracy. He is also a leader. Darryl Sutter says, "Jarome is the ideal leader."

The world of international hockey knows Jarome Iginla. Starting off with the World Juniors when he was just 18, he continued wearing the red and white maple leaf jersey in the Senior Men's World Championships, the 2004 World Cup and both the 2002 and 2006 Olympics. During his international tenure he has had his fair share of wins and losses which gives him the word "experienced" beside his name.

This Olympic team needs players who are experienced at winning the gold medal, and who know the feeling of what it is like to go home with the hardware. But never under estimate the power of a horrible loss. That sour taste is something no player wants to feel again. The devastating seventh place finish in the 2006 Winter Olympics, a team which Iginla captained, was not a good feeling and, it's safe to say, that all of the returning players from that team want some sort of redemption. Especially on home turf.

Iginla started his Junior career at 16 years old with the Kamloops Blazers of the WHL, in 1994. Kamloops had a strong team then, and in Iginla's rookie year, they won the Memorial Cup. Iginla picked up some points that season but he really made his name in the next season, 1994-95, when he scored

2009 August orientation camp

Home Ice

33 goals and 38 assists for a 71 point season. Then the Blazers, once again, made it to the Memorial Cup run. Iginla was a force, scoring five goals in the tournament to help the Blazers capture the Memorial Cup for a second year in a row. At the tournament, Iginla won the George Parsons Trophy for the most sportsmanlike player in the tournament. That spring he was drafted by the Dallas Stars as their first selection, eleventh overall. They didn't keep him long and on December 20 he was traded to the Calgary Flames, where he has become iconic.

The kind of trophy that Iginla won in the Juniors, for being a sportsmanlike player, was inevitable. Around the hockey scene, and to the public, Iginla is a nice guy, and extremely well respected. When playing in Toronto at the 2004 World Cup Series, one of the drivers commented that Jarome Iginla was so polite and always said thank you when he got out of the car after his ride.

Making this team, however, does boil down to what a player does on the ice. And according to the Hockey Canada management team, "Iginla does everything." But being a good guy is certainly helpful, as Iginla is easy to get along with, and coaches like that in a player.

Leadership and strength on the ice will take Jarome a long way toward his goal of once more playing for his country. Sure he has one Olympic gold medal, but even nice guys can be greedy.

Camp Highlights
Everyone knows that Jarome Iginla is a great player and that hitting is a big part of his game. The management team wanted to try him with Sidney Crosby and Rick Nash in the Red and White Game. Partway through the game he was taken off that line, but that doesn't really say too much. This was not an evaluation camp and Jarome has all fall to show his greatness.

Jarome was a key player for the 2004 World Cup Team, which Canada won with a flawless record.

Year	Team	Event	GP	G	A	PTS	PIM	Result
		Statistics– **International**						
		Regional						
1994	PAC	WU17						Bronze
		National						
1994	CAN	SU18	5	4	5	9	0	Gold
1996	CAN	WJC	6	2	0	2	10	Gold
1997	CAN	WHC	11	2	3	5	2	Gold
2002	CAN	OLY	6	3	1	4	0	Gold
2004	CAN	WC	6	2	1	3	2	1st
2006	CAN	OLY	6	2	1	3	4	7th
	CAN	INTL TOTAL	40	15	11	26	18	
	CAN	SR TOTAL	29	9	6	15	8	

VINCENT LECAVALIER

FORWARD #4

Shoots: **Left**
Height: **6'4"**
Weight: **215 lbs**
Birthdate: **April 21, 1980**
Birthplace: **Montreal, QC**
Hometown: **Île-Bizard, QC**
Team: **Tampa Bay Lightning (NHL)**
MHA: **AHM Lac St-Louis**
NHL Draft: **Tampa Bay Lightning: 1998 (1, 1)**
Last Amateur Club: **Rimouski Oceanic (QMJHL)**

CANADA

According to the Hockey Canada management team, Vincent Lecavalier definitely has the talent to play on the Canadian 2010 Olympic Squad, but, will he be healthy enough to play? The future for Lecavalier will depend on how he responds from his injuries. Based on his ability, he should be elite, but his biggest challenge will be in his recovery. Lecavalier is a solid goal scorer, with good hands, and he skates well for a 6'4" forward.

The title of elite hockey player suits Lecavalier because he is one of those players who has earned so many awards and accolades that the list goes on for pages. And it all started when he was a teenager. In his Junior career, Lecavalier played for the Rimouski Oceanic of the QMJHL. The first season he played with the team, he won the Michel Bergeron Trophy as the QMJHL's top rookie forward, plus he was awarded the CHL Rookie of the Year award, and was named to the CHL's All-Rookie Team.

One year later, in 1997-98 he won the QMJHL Top Prospect award. By now, the tongues were moving a million miles an hour as scouts talked about the kid named Lecavalier. When June, 1998, rolled around, and it was time for the NHL Entry Draft, everyone in the stands whispered about the new young sensation, Lecavalier. No one was surprised when his name was the very first called. He proudly stepped onto the stage and donned his Tampa Bay jersey, where he still plays today.

Less than two years after the draft, on March 11, 2000, Lecavalier was named the captain of Tampa, breaking a record to become the youngest captain in the NHL at just 19 years and 11 months. Since 2000, that record has been broken by, you guessed

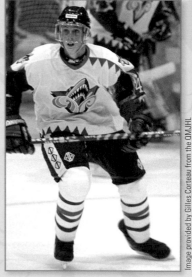

Vincent Lecavalier grew up in Quebec, where he played his Major Junior career. Here he is in a QMJHL Rimouski Oceanic jersey.

Image provided by Gilles Corteau from the QMJHL

Idol:
Tiger Woods

Favourite TV show:
Dexter

Favourite activities outside of hockey:
boating, golf

If not a hockey player would be a
Race Car Driver

Person who had most influence on
hockey career growing up:
dad

Favourite bands:
U2, Metallica

Hockey hero:
Steve Yzerman

Favourite team growing up:
Detroit Red Wings

2009 August orientation camp

Vincent Lecavalier

CANADA

it, Sidney Crosby. Lecavalier has played in four NHL all-star games, won the Maurice Richard Trophy and the King Clancy Trophy. And of course, who can forget the 2004 season, when Tampa Bay won the Stanley Cup? Having a Stanley Cup under his belt does make him a player who can be counted on to the win in a pressure situation.

Plus, he's collected some Hockey Canada accolades. His only big victory on a Canadian team came in 2004, when he played in the World Cup of Hockey in Toronto and won the Cup. That year, (get ready for this list), he led Canada in scoring, finished second overall in tournament scoring, was named to the World Cup's All-Tournament Team and was named the tournament MVP. What a sweep!

But let's get back to the injury that might keep this talented player from playing on the 2010 Olympic Team. On Friday, April 3, 2009, Lecavalier headed to Philadelphia to undergo arthroscopic surgery to his right wrist. Tampa's season was not yet finished but Lecavalier had been battling the pain for long enough and decided that he needed to have the surgery. He ended up missing the last five regular season games, playing a total of 77 games. It was the first time in six years that Lecavalier didn't score 30 goals in the season. It might have had something to do with his shoulder injury from the previous summer that hindered him from training. With the shoulder injury healed, Lecavalier definitely hit bad luck when he injured his right wrist. Healing time for his most-recent surgery is expected to only be four to six weeks.

The verdict on Lecavalier is not out yet and the Hockey Canada management team will be watching him in the fall. Like they have said, "he has all the tools to be dominant but his challenge will be in his recovery."

Camp Highlights
The coaches liked the way Lecavalier played at camp, how he skated and moved the puck. His camp was great; his game was good. For the game he was on a line with Smyth and Sharp.

Tampa Bay Lightning

Home Ice

Here is an intense Lecavalier at the 2004 World Cup Championship in Toronto.

Statistics– **International**								
Year	Team	Event	GP	G	A	PTS	PIM	Result
Regional								
1997	QC	WU17	4	2	3	5	12	Bronze
National								
1997	CAN	SU18	-	-	-	-	-	Gold
1998	CAN	WJC	7	1	1	2	4	8th
2001	CAN	WHC	7	3	2	5	29	5th
2004	CAN	WC	6	2	5	7	8	1st
2006	CAN	OLY	6	0	3	3	16	7th
	CAN	INTL TOTAL	26	6	11	17	57	
	CAN	SR TOTAL	19	5	10	15	53	

Vincent Lecavalier

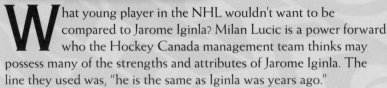

MILAN LUCIC

FORWARD #17

Shoots: **Left**
Height: **6'3"**
Weight: **228 lbs**
Birthdate: **June 7, 1988**
Birthplace: **Vancouver, B.C.**
Hometown: **Vancouver, B.C.**
Team: **Boston Bruins (NHL)**
MHA: **Vancouver Thunderbirds MHA**
NHL Draft: **Boston Bruins: 2006 (2, 50)**
Last Amateur Club: **Vancouver Giants (WHL)**

What young player in the NHL wouldn't want to be compared to Jarome Iginla? Milan Lucic is a power forward who the Hockey Canada management team thinks may possess many of the strengths and attributes of Jarome Iginla. The line they used was, "he is the same as Iginla was years ago."

When Lucic made the roster, the media speculated as to why when other players, like Stephen Stamkos, were not there. Okay, so he has some Igilina qualities. Is that enough?

He's only been in the NHL for two years, starting on the Bruins lineup in 2007-08. It was in the 2008-09 season that he picked his game up a notch and scored 17 goals for 42 points in 72 games. But even that probably wouldn't have been enough for Hockey Canada to want him on the roster. Clearly, it was his vision in the 2009 playoffs that really showed what Lucic was made of, catching the scouts' eyes. In game five of the Bruins second playoff series against Carolina, Lucic set the tone of the game by stepping on the ice and being physical from the moment the puck was dropped. The Bruins crowd loved his big hits and his committed energy. He definitely helped the Bruins win that game 4-0. During the Bruins playoff run, he scored three goals for nine points. Lucic showed the hockey world that he had good hands, not to mention his physical presence.

When Lucic got the phone call that he was on the orientation camp roster, he was probably a bit stunned. Six years ago, in 2003, Lucic wanted to quit playing hockey after his name was nowhere on the list in the WHL Bantam Draft. Then he got an invite to play for the Burnaby Express Junior 'A' club but didn't get past the rookie camp. Disheartened, he played Junior B. As the season progressed,

Milan Lucic played his minor hockey career with the Vancouver Thunderbirds Minor Hockey Association. Here he is in his early, early years.

Image provided by Gerry Johannson

Home Ice

Other sports:
lacrosse, baseball

Hockey hero:
Jarome Iginla

Favourite TV show:
Seinfeld

Favourite activity
outside of hockey:
music

If not a hockey player would be a:
policeman

Favourite band:
Metallica

Favourite team growing up:
Vancouver Canucks

Favourite book:
Harry Potter series

Boston Bruins

Milan Lucic

CANADA

Lucic was called on to play with the Express. From there he let all his thoughts about quitting go and he worked to get better and better.

His actions paid off. The next season, he moved up to Major Junior, playing on the Vancouver Giants, and helping them to a WHL title. When June rolled around, he was selected fiftieth overall by the Boston Bruins in the 2006 NHL Entry Draft.

This gave him a boost, and when Lucic hit the ice in September with the Vancouver Giants, he found his stride. Quickly, he became one of the Giant's best players and by the end of the season he had won the scoring race with 68 points. The Giants went to game seven of the Memorial Cup, losing a heart-breaker to Medicine Hat.

Revenge is sweet and even sweeter on home ice. Vancouver won the bid to host the Memorial Cup in 2007 and in the final match-up, the Giants were once again playing Medicine Hat. They won the Memorial Cup that year, and Lucic won the Stafford Smythe Memorial Trophy for the Memorial Cup MVP. In addition, he made the Memorial Cup All-Star Team. Not bad for a kid who wanted to quit. Oh yeah, and that same year, he won Vancouver's MVP plus he also won the team's humanitarian award for his services in the community.

With only two years playing in the NHL beside his name, Lucic is that kid who is "learning the ropes." Hockey Canada likes him. His only claim to fame playing internationally was in August-September of 2007 when he played on Canada's National Junior Team in the Canada-Russia Super Series. For the event he wore the "C."

Lucic is a young and up-and-coming physical player, who is showing great signs of being a power forward and a goal scorer. Can he be that player on the 2010 Olympic squad that perhaps plays on the fourth line, but gets the crowd going with his huge hits?

Camp Highlights

Milan Lucic likes to play for the big hits and the camp and the Red and White game didn't showcase what he is capable of. But he still showed that he was definitely worthy of being invited to the camp and playing in big games.

2009 August orientation camp

134

Statistics– **International**

Year	Team	Event	GP	G	A	PTS	PIM	Result
		Regional						
		Not applicable						
		National						
2007	CAN	SS	8	0	3	3	12	1st
	CAN	INTL TOTAL	8	0	3	3	12	
	CAN	SR TOTAL	0	0	0	0	0	

Milan Lucic was the captain of the 2007 Canada/ Russia Super Series Team. Here he is hoisting the cup.

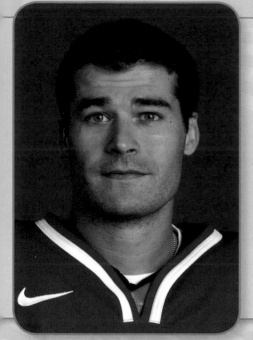

PATRICK MARLEAU

FORWARD #12

Shoots: **Left**
Height: **6'2"**
Weight: **220 lbs**
Birthdate: **September 15, 1979**
Birthplace: **Swift Current, Sask.**
Hometown: **Aneroid, Sask.**
Team: **San Jose Sharks (NHL)**
MHA: **Aneroid MHA**
NHL Draft: **San Jose Sharks: 1997 (1, 2)**
Last Amateur Club: **Seattle Thunderbirds (WHL)**

Considered to be the fastest skater on the roster, Patrick Marleau was a sure thing when it came to selecting the camp. It helped that Marleau also had a phenomenal year with the San Jose Sharks in 2008-09. He is what the Hockey Canada management team dubs as "loyal."

As a multiple task player, Marleau is known to be able to play centre or wing and be equally as good at both. He's one of those players who can play up and down the lineup. In the top group of forwards, he can score, or down as the thirteenth forward, he can be the energy guy. He's versatile, and is that "anywhere" player that is so needed in international hockey.

Let's talk about his 2008-09 season. He scored a record high amount of goals at 38 for a total of 71 points, but this didn't pass his career point total which actually happened in the 2005-06 season.

Marleau had a bit of a down season in 2007-08, so when he came out flying in 2008-09, Hockey Canada was pleased to see his enhanced performance. Slumps are difficult to overcome at times, but Marleau put forth a strong effort to get back to where he had been. The extra six goals definitely made a difference. In the Hockey Canada discussion about Marleau one of the more specific comments was noting his effectiveness in cycling the puck in the offensive zone. He did that well in his 2008-09 season.

Marleau has played in three NHL All-Star games (2004, 2007 and 2009), and over the years he's had his fair share of awards. Like a lot of players on this roster, Marleau started his career in Major Junior and was a top Junior player. In 1997, when he was playing for

This photo was taken in 1991 when Patrick Marleau was 12 years old and playing with Swift Current.

Hockey hero:
Mario Lemieux

Favourite activities
outside of hockey:
golf, family activities

If not a hockey player would be a:
**pro baseball player
or accountant**

Person who had most influence on
hockey career growing up:
Dad

Favourite band:
Nickelback

Most memorable
minor hockey experience:
**winning championship
in Atom**

Favourite team growing up:
Pittsburgh Penguins

Favourite book:
**Payne Stewart:
The Authorized Biography**

Patrick Marleau played for
Canada in the 2003 IIHF Men's
World Championship in Finland.
Canada won the gold medal.

Patrick Marleau

the Seattle Thunderbirds, he was named to the WHL West First All-Star Team.

That accolade carried him into his Draft year, and Marleau went second overall in the 1997 NHL Entry Draft to the San Jose Sharks. He made his debut with the Sharks in the 1997-98 season under head coach Darryl Sutter. The experienced Sutter knew what to do with Marleau. Besides working on his great offensive talents, Darryl shaped Marleau into a more defensively minded and an all-around player.

This all-around player is looking good for the Olympic team as this kind of player is versatile and accountable.

Right from the beginning, Marleau was a steady player for the Sharks. For his first seven years, he played well and made a name for himself. His real superstardom, however, came right after the 2004-05 lockout. Marleau took the year off, rather than playing in Europe like so many of his NHL brethren and when the teams returned to the ice for the 2005-06 season, Marleau's year of hiatus left him rested and ready to play with a renewed energy. The new league rules helped him because he was such a strong, fast efficient skater and suddenly, he was able to blow by the opposition with his speed. In his record high in that 2005-06 season, Marleau scored 34 goals and 52 assists for 86 points in 82 games.

Marleau has successful international experience. He has played in a number of tournaments for Team Canada and earned a gold

San Jose Sharks

medal and a World Cup title to boast about for his efforts. From the 2004 World Cup in Toronto and the 2003 World Championships in Finland, Marleau learned the level of intensity needed to win internationally. In 2006, Marleau was invited to the Olympic orientation camp in August but when the final roster was announced in December, his name was not on it. This disappointment will undoubtedly motivate him to work that much harder this fall to maintain the attention of Team Canada management. This is something he wants. Watch him in the fall of 2009-10, and see what he can do.

Camp Highlights

Patrick Marleau picked up the second goal for Team Red in the second period and it was unassisted. Prior to that, he had assisted on Jeff Carter's goal— the first Team Red goal. Then in the shootout, he sunk a nice shot to beat Fleury. Overall, Marleau had a great game.

2009 August orientation camp

Statistics– **International**								
Year	Team	Event	GP	G	A	PTS	PIM	Result
Regional								
1995	SK	CWG			unavailable			Gold
National								
1996	CAN	SU18	5	3	3	6	8	Gold
1999	CAN	WHC	7	1	2	3	0	4th
2001	CAN	WHC	7	2	3	5	4	5th
2003	CAN	WHC	9	0	4	4	4	Gold
2004	CAN	WC	-	-	-	-	-	1st
2005	CAN	WHC	9	2	2	4	4	Silver
	CAN	INTL TOTAL	37	8	14	22	20	
	CAN	SR TOTAL	32	5	11	16	12	

ANDY MCDONALD

FORWARD #10

Shoots : **Left**
Height: **5'11"**
Weight: **183 lbs**
Birthdate: **August 25, 1977**
Birthplace: **Strathroy, Ont.**
Hometown: **Strathroy, Ont.**
Team: **St. Louis Blues (NHL)**
MHA: **Strathroy MHA**
NHL Draft: **Undrafted**
Last Amateur Club: **Colgate University (ECAC)**

CANADA

A nother speedy forward, Andy McDonald has great quickness in small spaces. McDonald is one of the smaller forwards (5'11" 183 lbs), but he is a dangerous scoring player because of his ability to shift, move, and find those small openings on the ice. McDonald is a versatile forward that can play either wing or centre and play both extremely well. He's what the Hockey Canada management team classified as a "utility guy."

Born in 1977, Andy was one of the older players at camp, though despite his years in hockey, he has only played on one Hockey Canada team—the 2002 team that travelled to Sweden to play in the IIHF World Championship.

He also was one of the few at this orientation camp who is undrafted.

As a teenager, McDonald played Junior B hockey. Not Major Junior like most players on the list, or even Junior 'A', but Junior B. His route to the NHL was definitely different than most of the other forwards on the roster. Obviously, he is one of those players who kept his dream alive year after year, continuing to plug away and practising his skills. Power skating lessons and perseverance have paid off for this athlete as impressive skating is something that defines him. As a young kid and a teenager, McDonald always knew that there were a lot of skeptics who doubted that he would ever make it in the NHL. Size was his weakness, but speed was his strength and he learned how to use it effectively.

During his time playing with the Strathroy Rockets Junior B club, McDonald was one of their best players. In 1994-95 he was named the Rockets MVP, and he also received the Eastern Division

Image provided by Andy McDonald

Christmas was joyful for a young Andy McDonald because he got a lot of hockey gear.

2009 August orientation camp

Favourite TV show:
House

Favourite activity outside of hockey:
boating

If not a hockey player would be a:
construction worker

Person who had most influence on
hockey career growing up:
Dad

Favourite band:
Dave Matthews Band

Hockey hero:
Wayne Gretzky

Favourite team growing up:
Toronto Maple Leafs

Favourite book:
**Water for Elephants by
Sarah Gruen**

Andy Mcdonald

MVP, League MVP, and the OHA Player of the Year from the Ontario Hockey Association (OHA).

Continuing his success the following season (1995-96), McDonald picked up many of the final awards including the Playoff MVP. It was during the playoffs that he was scouted by Colgate University, founded in 1819, and located in Hamilton, New York. Four years of College Hockey gave McDonald a lot of time to grow and mature as a player. McDonald ended up being a two-time all-ECAC Hockey selection and is still tied for sixteenth in Colgate's all-time scoring list. In 137 games, he produced 67 goals, and 87 assists. In his senior year of college, he was instrumental in helping his team to a 24-9-2 season. For his efforts that year, McDonald was named a first-team all-league honouree, and he was a finalist for the Hobey Baker Memorial Award, which is given to the nation's top men's Collegiate Hockey player.

When it was McDonald's draft year, he went undrafted. Most players in this situation might throw in the towel, but not McDonald. In 2000, he signed as a free agent with Anaheim. He moved up and down between the NHL and the AHL, scoring here and there, and picking up some assists along the way.

During the 2004-05 lockout, McDonald spent his season playing in Europe. Then a new season arrived, and a new NHL emerged because of the new rules. Because of the increased flow of the game, McDonald was able to show off his speed. In that first year after the lockout, McDonald played 82 games with Anaheim and scored 34 goals, 51 assists for a grand total of 85 points. He had raised his points total from 30 to 85. This 55 point spread put McDonald on a page with some of the best players in the NHL.

Two years later, on January 19, 2007, McDonald was invited to play in his first NHL All-Star competition. Going against the best players in the NHL in the skills competition, McDonald won the fastest skater challenge.

Then in the same year that he won that award, McDonald played extremely well, earning a first star award in game four of the Stanley Cup finals, helping the Anaheim Ducks when they made their run for the

St. Louis Blues

Here is Andy playing in the 2002 IIHF Men's World Championship against the USA. The tournament took place in Sweden.

Stanley Cup. Later that year, on December 14, 2007, McDonald was traded to the St. Louis Blues.

Yes, McDonald took an unconventional path to get into the NHL and be named as one of Canada's orientation camp players for 2010. He is also a great penalty killer and will be watched in the early part of the 2009 season.

Camp Highlights

Andy McDonald looked creative during the ice sessions, and during the Red and White game. He also showed that he had good, quick hands. Playing centre, he started off with Cleary and Lucic as his wingers but because Gagne was missing from the lineup he was moved around to play with other wingers. Competition is fierce for the centremen on this team.

		Statistics– **International**						
Year	Team	Event	GP	G	A	PTS	PIM	Result
		Regional						
		Not applicable						
		National						
2002	CAN	WHC	7	4	1	5	0	6th
	CAN	INTL TOTAL	7	4	1	5	0	
	CAN	SR TOTAL	7	4	1	5	0	

Andy Mcdonald

BRENDEN MORROW

FORWARD #10

Shoots: **Left**
Height: **5'11"**
Weight: **205 lbs**
Birthdate: **January 16, 1979**
Birthplace: **Arcola, Sask.**
Hometown: **Carlyle, Sask.**
Team: **Dallas Stars (NHL)**
MHA: **Carlyle MHA**
NHL Draft : **Dallas Stars: 1997 (1, 25)**
Last Amateur Club: **Portland Winter Hawks (WHL)**

CANADA

On November 20, 2008, when the Dallas Stars were playing the Chicago Blackhawks at home, Stars captain, Brenden Morrow suffered a blow to his knee. A tough player, he didn't think it was all that bad—he could walk on it—but the doctors thought otherwise. Morrow tore his anterior cruciate ligament in his right knee, and needed surgery. His estimated recovery time: six months.

This news rocked the Stars franchise, not to mention their fans. Morrow had been on a roll and was, by far, their best player. In just 18 games he'd scored five goals and 10 assists. Hoping to come back for the playoffs, Morrow was disappointed when the Stars didn't make it that far in 2009, and he didn't play another game that season. The team seemed to be missing something without Morrow, perhaps his energy, enthusiasm, and passion for the game. He's a player who is known to play with his heart game after game.

The fact that Morrow hasn't played since November, didn't stop the 2010 Hockey Canada management team from putting his name on the roster for the August orientation camp. Morrow is a great power forward who has the uncanny ability to score in close making him a constant producer of goals and assists. For a player who measures in at just 5'11" he's tough, and certainly doesn't back down from a confrontation even when there are times when he should. One of his best attributes—and one that the folks at Hockey Canada really liked—is his work along the boards. Morrow is not afraid to get dirty to come up with the puck, and he is that "down low" player. Sometimes, that kind of play can produce injuries.

Image provided by Jason Rademan of the Dallas Stars

A young Brendan Morrow when he played minor hockey in Saskatchewan. He played for the Carlyle MHA.

Home Ice

2009 August orientation camp

Idol:
Tiger Woods

Favourite TV show:
Entourage

Favourite activity outside
of hockey:
golf

Person who had most influence on
hockey career growing up:
parents

Best concerts ever attended:
Elton John, Billy Joel

Hockey hero:
Brett Hull

Favourite team growing up:
Calgary Flames

Favourite book:
**Angels and Demons,
Dan Brown**

Brenden Morrow

CANADA

For three consecutive years with the Portland Winter Hawks in the WHL, Morrow scored over 85 points. Naturally, he went high in the 1997 NHL Entry Draft. The Dallas Stars picked this young, talented Junior player in the first round, twenty-fifth overall. He didn't make the immediate jump to the NHL, and spent another year in Junior. The next season proved to be a good one for Morrow because the Portland Winter Hawks made it to the Memorial Cup finals. The Memorial Cup experience helped Morrow make his leap to the NHL and he easily adapted to playing with the big boys.

In his first few years with Dallas, he was a consistent player and grabbed points here and there, spanning from 33- 49. Then the lockout arrived, and when it was over, the new rules were in effect. A power forward like Morrow capitalized on the new game, and became a goal-getter. That year, he recorded his best season ever with 23 goals, and 42 assists for a total of 65 points. It was also the year that he emerged as a tough, gritty-along-the-boards, feisty player, chalking up 183 penalty minutes. His positive plus/minus in his first six years of playing with the Stars, combined with managing to steadily earn points, helped him become their captain.

The Olympic dream is alive for Brenden Morrow. In 2002 he attended the Olympic orientation camp but was not named to their roster. He was also not on the 2006 Olympic roster. But he has done some time for Hockey Canada, having played on six teams over the years,

2009 August orientation camp

starting with the World Junior Team in 1999, winning a silver medal in Winnipeg. As a late addition to the Men's World Championship team in 2001, Morrow flew over to Germany, only to play up to the quarter-final game. The elimination stung. And it didn't get any better the following year, in 2002, when the Men's World Team had another horrible performance. He has one gold medal from the 2004 IIHF Men's World Championship and he was also on the 2004 World Cup Team that came out victorius and won the Cup. He has one lone silver medal from the 2005 Men's World Championship.

If Brenden Morrow is healthy, and his knee holds up during the first half of the season, he could very well be a contender for the 2010 Men's Olympic Team.

Camp Highlights

During the camp, and at the Red and White game, Brendan Morrow seemed to fit in quite nicely with Michael Richards and Jeff Carter. He also wowed the crowd when he scored in the shootout.

Dallas Stars

Statistics– International

Year	Team	Event	GP	G	A	PTS	PIM	Result
		Regional						
1995	WEST	WU17	6	2	3	5	20	4th
		National						
1999	CAN	WJC	7	1	7	8	4	Silver
2001	CAN	WHC	1	0	0	0	0	5th
2002	CAN	WHC	7	0	1	1	2	6th
2004	CAN	WHC	9	1	6	7	6	Gold
2004	CAN	WHC	1	0	0	0	4	Gold
2005	CAN	WHC	9	0	1	1	6	Silver
	CAN	INTL TOTAL	34	2	15	17	22	
	CAN	SR TOTAL	27	1	8	9	18	

RICK NASH

FORWARD #61

Shoots: **Left**
Height: **6'4"**
Weight: **218 lbs**
Birthdate: **June 16, 1984**
Birthplace: **Brampton, Ont.**
Hometown: **Brampton, Ont.**
Team: **Columbus Blue Jackets (NHL)**
MHA: **Toronto Marlboros**
NHL Draft: **Columbus Blue Jackets: 2002 (1, 1)**
Last Amateur Club: **London Knights (OHL)**

One of the bigger forwards on the roster, Rick Nash at 6'4" and 220 lbs, is a player who works down low and uses his strength and size at the hash marks. At the faceoff circle, when the puck is dropped, he pushes and shoves to get control. Good at protecting the puck, he drives hard to the net, and is sometimes impossible to stop because of his large presence. His dominating size, combined with his good skating skills and a wicked shot, make Nash a player who can create a tremendous amount of offence. It also helps that he is constantly aware of his defenders and has great vision in knowing where they are.

Throughout Nash's NHL career with the Columbus Blue Jackets, Coach Ken Hitchcock has worked on his abilities both on and off the ice. He made him captain. To look at him, one would never know that behind the scenes, Nash is a quiet and reserved individual who is trying hard to learn to be more vocal as a captain. Most people assume that guys like him should be extroverted, bigger than life, full of testosterone and brawn. The word is out that he is becoming more and more vocal every year in the dressing room, a learned response to his coach's direction. Rick has definitely grown with his role as captain.

On the ice, Nash is used in many different ways. Because he reads the play well and is offensive in the defensive zone, Hitchcock has used him as a penalty killer. But will Team Canada?

In the 2008-09 season, he did score a number of short-handed goals just by reading and reacting and moving the puck out of the zone. Two-way players like Nash go a long way because of the

Rick Nash getting ready to fire the puck at the 2002 IIHF World Junior Championship.

Idols:
parents, brother

Favourite TV shows:
Seinfeld, Family Guy

Favourite activity outside hockey:
boating

If not a hockey player would be a:
policeman or a gym teacher

Person who had most influence on
hockey career growing up:
parents, Keith Kerrigan

Favourite band:
Green Day

Favourite team growing up:
Toronto Maple Leafs

Favourite book:
**Of Mice and Men by
John Steinback**

2009 August orientation camp

Rick Nash

many roles they can play and the depth that they bring to the game. Nash is a player who has learned how to be responsible.

Of course, he also comes to the team with international experience. In 2002, in his second year of Junior with the London Knights, Nash was chosen for the IIHF World Junior Team. Although he only scored three points and the team took home a silver medal, the experience helped him learn what is needed to play international hockey and to play it well.

In 2005, he took a leap internationally and made the IIHF World Championship Team that played in Vienna, Austria. Again he brought home the silver medal. Just six months later, Nash made the coveted 2006 Olympic Team that was to play in Turin, Italy. Disappointed and disillusioned, Nash came home from Turin, Italy with his seventh place finish.

Fortunately, a gold medal was right around the corner for Nash. In 2007, when the wounds from the Olympics had turned to scars, Nash once again made the IIHF World Championship Team and flew over to Moscow. It was a sweet victory for Nash because he scored two goals in the final gold medal game against Finland for a total of 11 points in the tournament. He was named to the tournament All-Star Team, earning some big MVP honours.

In the world of hockey, players must take the good with the bad. Sometimes on-ice mistakes are made and games are lost. In 2008, in front of the home town Canadian crowd in Quebec—this was a first ever for the IIHF World Championships to be played in Canada—Nash took a delay of game penalty in the final gold medal game, in the overtime period. The score was tied 4-4. Canada had let a decent two-goal lead swish down the drain so what happened next wasn't all on Nash's shoulders. Minutes into the overtime period, Nash

Columbus Blue Jackets

accidentally shot the puck over the glass as he was attempting to clear it from the Canadian zone. Russia, who had scored two unanswered goals while the Canadians were skating on their heels, took full advantage of the power play to defeat Canada 5-4. Yes, Nash had slipped up and made a grave error but he was still named to the tournament All-Star Team and recorded 13 points in the tournament.

All of this experience—good and bad—is important and gives Rick Nash character, depth, drive, and determination. It will make Nash a smarter player with a vendetta to win and win big. Mentally and physically Nash is ready to play for gold with this 2010 Olympic Team.

2009 August orientation camp

Camp Highlights

Rick Nash and Sidney Crosby played most of the Red and White game together and they were also paired in the ice sessions. Crosby was centre and Nash over on the wing. This duo showed signs of great chemistry.

Year	Team	Event	GP	G	A	PTS	PIM	Result
				Statistics– International				
		Regional						
2001	ON	WU17	4	5	2	7	6	Bronze
		National						
2001	CAN	SU18	4	5	5	10	2	Gold
2002	CAN	WJC	7	1	2	3	2	Silver
2005	CAN	WHC	9	9	6	15	8	Silver
2006	CAN	OLY	6	0	1	1	10	7th
2007	CAN	WHC	9	6	5	11	4	Gold
2008	CAN	WHC	9	6	7	13	6	Silver
	CAN	INTL TOTAL	44	27	26	53	32	
	CAN	SR TOTAL	33	21	19	40	28	

Rick Nash

COREY PERRY

FORWARD #10

Shoots: **Right**
Height: **6'3"**
Weight: **209 lbs**
Birthdate: **May 16, 1985**
Birthplace: **New Liskeard, Ont.**
Hometown: **Peterborough, Ont.**
Team: **Anaheim Ducks (NHL)**
MHA: **Peterborough MHA**
NHL Draft: **Anaheim Ducks: 2003 (1, 28)**
Last Amateur Club: **London Knights (OHL)**

When some players step onto the ice together, they possess immediate chemistry. Corey Perry and Ryan Getzlaf are a great pair, and they have that mysterious, unpredictable chemistry that is so important in any team sport. This duo has been noticed by the Hockey Canada management team. Individually, they are both solid contenders for the team, but together they are even stronger.

Perry is a bit of a dichotomy because he's smooth and rough. His soft hands help him score goals, but he also has a razor side that gives him that ability to play with an edge. Some have toted him as an "agitator" and a real disturber. Right now, Perry is classified as that "new breed of player," one who possesses offensive talent but is tough, and plays a defensive push and shove game that creates penalties for the opposition.

This young man was only in his second season in the NHL when he first earned the honour of hoisting the Stanley Cup above his head in the Duck's 2007 victory. But the best part for Perry was that he was deserving of the honour. He had been instrumental in helping Anaheim win. At the time, Brian Burke was the GM of the Ducks and he said, "Corey is one of the top young players in the NHL today. He's a true Duck, a hard-nosed goal scorer who's difficult to play against." He had scored 44 points (17 goals, 27 assists) in the regular season but he flourished in the playoffs by gathering 15 points in 21 games. Not bad for a kid who was only in his second year with an NHL franchise, and his first year playing the full schedule.

During Anaheim's run to the cup, Perry played with Getzlaf and Dustin Penner; they were known as the "kid line." This,

Image provided by Dan Hamilton/OHL

Corey Perry picking up awards at the OHL Awards banquet in 2004 when he played for the London Knights.

2009 August orientation camp

Idol:
Tiger Woods

Favourite TV show:
Prison Break

Favourite activity outside of hockey:
camping

If not a hockey player would be a:
golfer or teacher

Person who had most influence on
hockey career growing up:
parents

Most memorable
minor hockey experience:
**playing in All-Ontario's in
Major Bantam**

Hockey Hero:
Joe Sakic

Favourite team growing up:
Montreal Canadiens

Corey Perry

however, was not Perry's first introduction to playing with Getzlaf. They were both rookies for the Anaheim Ducks in 2005-06 and when they were sent down to play in the AHL, they became linemates. In combination they scored 67 points in 36 games with the Portland Pirates. They made such a name for themselves that it wasn't long before they were called back up to play with the Ducks.

Perry came to the Ducks in 2003, when they drafted him in the first round twenty-eighth overall. Prior to his draft year, Perry played for the London Knights of the OHL. In his fourth and last season with the Knights, he recorded a personal best of 130 points in just 60 regular season games. Then he went on to pick up 38 more points in the playoffs as his team became the OHL champion, giving them the berth to make a run for the Memorial Cup, which they won.

Even though he is young, he has played in big tournaments and knows how to play in stressful playoff situations. Hockey Canada recognizes what a player must contribute to a team to capture a Memorial Cup and to win a Stanley Cup, so next to Perry's name on the management's spread sheet is mention of these successes.

His Hockey Canada experience would not fill a page or even a couple of lines as he has only been on one team but if you count his Under-18 stint, then his credit rating rises to two teams. The one team he played for internationally was the dominant, gold-medal winning, 2005 IIHF World Junior Team. Perry was a heavy contributor to

Anaheim Ducks

Corey Perry skating by his opponent when he played at the 2005 IIHF World Junior Championship in North Dakota. Canada took home gold.

the team's big victory as he played on the first line with Sidney Crosby and Patrice Bergeron.

For a young guy he has experience and he has size. He has enough toughness that he is slotted as a player who isn't afraid to mix it up and play gritty hockey. Hockey Canada needs players who have an edge. Will the line combination of Perry and Getzlaf be a determining factor in the big decision?

Camp Highlights
Corey Perry scored the second goal for Team White, showing that he doesn't always need Ryan Getzlaf to look good. With Ryan Getzlaf out of the lineup, Corey Perry was slotted, for the most part, with Eric Staal and Jason Spezza.

Statistics– **International**								
Year	Team	Event	GP	G	A	PTS	PIM	Result
		Regional						
2002	ONT	WU17	6	4	2	6	12	Bronze
		National						
2002	CAN	SU18	5	5	5	10	6	Gold
2005	CAN	WJC	6	2	5	7	6	Gold
	CAN	INTL TOTAL	11	7	10	17	12	
	CAN	SR TOTAL	0	0	0	0	0	

MICHAEL RICHARDS

FORWARD #18

Shoots: **Left**
Height: **5'11"**
Weight: **195 lbs**
Birthdate: **February 11, 1985**
Birthplace: **Kenora, Ont.**
Hometown: **Kenora, Ont.**
Team: **Philadelphia Flyers (NHL)**
MHA: **Kenora (ON) Stars**
NHL Draft : **Philadelphia Flyers: 2003 (1, 24)**
Last Amateur Club: **Kitchener Rangers (OHL)**

A good work ethic on the ice and leadership off of the ice are characteristics that are rewarded. Of course, some skill has to go along with those outstanding character traits. No player can make an Olympic camp roster without having excellent skills.

Known for his hard work and consistent effort, Michael Richards is a crafty player who the critics say has, "great vision on the ice." Perhaps he doesn't have those soft hands that label so many players, but he has the grit to get the job done, and knows how to pick up a loose puck in front of the net. A goal is a goal. He's also known as a good two-way player, which puts him in a special category.

Richards is considered somewhat small at 5'11" and 195 lbs. This lack in size, however, doesn't stop him from going in the corners with the bigger players, fighting for the puck, and more often than not, coming out with it on the end of his stick. He takes a hit and can give one too. The Hockey Canada management team has compared him to Bobby Clarke.

His title, according to the Hockey Canada management team, is a "completely skilled player." In other words, he has a little bit of everything. Over the years he has been criticized for his skating strength but the fact that he gets to the net for the loose pucks makes up for any lack in stride.

Richards is also one of those players who is a natural leader and has captained a fair share of teams in his short career. Last fall, he was named the captain of the Philadelphia Flyers. Prior to that, he captained the IIHF World Junior Team in 2005 that won the gold medal in North Dakota and he was also named an alternate captain for the IIHF Men's World team in 2006 when they played in Latvia.

Michael Richards talking to a reporter after a game in 2003 when he played in the OHL with the Kitchener Rangers.

2009 August orientation camp

Hockey hero:
Joe Sakic

Favourite TV show:
Two and a Half Men

Favourite activity outside of hockey:
boating

If not a hockey player would be a:
teacher

Person who had most influence on
hockey career growing up:
parents

Favourite music artist:
Eminem

Favourite team growing up:
Winnipeg Jets

Favourite book:
**Josh Hamilton biography—
Beyond Belief:
Finding the Strength to
Come Back**

Michael Richards

For Team Canada, Richards also played in the 2004 IIHF World Junior Championship, winning a silver medal. The Team Canada management team has made notes about his leadership strengths and how he is a "good captain."

The Hockey Canada management team looks at experience as a necessary ingredient because it lets them see who can play in pressure situations and who can last physically and emotionally. Although he is not a Stanley Cup champion like so many players on the roster, Richards is a player with some hard-core experience. Along with his gold medal at World Juniors, he has a Memorial Cup and a Calder Cup beside his name.

Richards' Memorial Cup victory came in 2003 when he was playing for the dominating Kitchener Rangers. Only in his second year, he managed to capture the regular season scoring title for his team by registering a proud 87 points. Heading into the draft that spring, general managers questioned his size but he still went in the first round, twenty-fourth overall. There were players who went higher than Richards, who were bigger, but hadn't produced like he had in that Junior year.

Here is Richards holding the trophy over his head at the 2005 IIHF World Junior Championship in Grand Forks, North Dakota.

In his last year of Juniors, Richards's team made another run for the Memorial Cup, but failed to go the distance. In just 15 games, Richards had his name on the game sheet 28 times. Shortly after the Rangers were eliminated, Richards was called to play for the Philadelphia Phantoms, the Flyers' AHL team. This proved to be a good call-up for Richards. Scoring over a point a game, Richards aided the Phantoms as they sealed the Calder Cup.

Small, but tough, Richards is one of those important players who gets recognized for his skills on the ice as well as for his leadership skills. Consistently good, he plays hard every time he steps on the ice. Richards will certainly get a good look in the fall when he suits up to play another year with the Philadelphia Flyers.

Camp Highlights

In the Red and White game, Michael Richards assisted on Jeff Carter's goal, which was the first Red goal of the night. Again, competition for the centres is really tough, but Richards played well at camp, and is in definite contention for one of the centre spots.

Philadelphia Flyers

Statistics– **International**								
Year	Team	Event	GP	G	A	PTS	PIM	Result
			Regional					
			Not applicable					
2002	ON	WU17	6	2	6	8	0	Bronze
			National					
2002	CAN	SU18	5	3	3	6	2	Gold
2004	CAN	WJC	6	2	3	5	2	Silver
2005	CAN	WJC	6	1	4	5	2	Gold
2006	CAN	WHC	9	3	2	5	10	4th
	CAN	INTL TOTAL	26	9	12	21	16	
	CAN	SR TOTAL	9	3	2	5	10	

Michael Richards

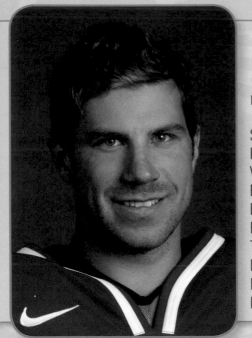

DEREK ROY

FORWARD #9

Shoots: **Left**
Height: **5'9"**
Weight: **188 lbs**
Birthdate: **May 4, 1983**
Birthplace: **Ottawa, Ont.**
Hometown: **Rockland, Ont.**
Team: **Buffalo Sabres (NHL)**
MHA: **Clarence MHA**
NHL Draft/ : **Buffalo Sabres: 2001 (2, 32)**
Last Amateur Club: **Kitchener Rangers (OHL)**

There's small, those players who register around 5'11", then there's smaller, those players around 5'10", and then there's smallest—5'9" and under. Okay, smallest only applies to a handful of players who have beaten the odds, ignored the critics, and stuck with a dream that most would have told them was clearly not in their future.

Derek Roy is one of those players. How do these little guys make it to the NHL? Multi-dimensional, Roy can play any position on the forward line: right, left, centre. No matter what position the coaches tell him to play, he plays strong. One-on-one, he can play with anyone. He makes clever passes and has spent years honing his stick-handling skills so he can weave around the big guys. Feisty is a word that is often used to describe Roy. Obviously, he is fearless. Any 5'9" player who is willing to step on the ice with guys who are 6'4" cannot have one ounce of fear.

He has often been compared to Theo Fleury and Martin St. Louis.

In the 1999-00 season, when Roy was just 17 years old he played for the Kitchener Rangers of the OHL. In 66 games he scored 34 goals for 87 points and this gave him a front row seat on the OHL All-Rookie Team. He was talented from a young age. It's slightly easier to make a Major Junior team as a small player, but the odds are diminished when a smaller player tries to make the big leagues.

Roy didn't let his size predict his outcome. A strong player for a strong team, Roy continued with the Kitchener Rangers for another four years. In his second year he scored 42 goals and 81 points, which was enough to have his name called at the 2001 NHL Entry draft.

Derek Roy played on the 2003 IIHF World Junior Championship Team in Halifax, Nova Scotia.

2009 August
orientation camp

Idol:
Michael Jordan

Favourite TV show:
Entourage

Favourite activity outside of hockey:
boating

Person who had most influence on
hockey career growing up:
Dad

Favourite band:
Metallica

Hockey hero:
Steve Yzerman

Favourite magazine:
Architectural Digest

Favourite book:
**21:Bringing the House
Down by Ben Mezrich**

Derek Roy

CANADA

The Buffalo Sabres picked him up thirty-second overall. Continuing to be the Rangers top scorer, Roy hoped to have some success at the Sabres training camp. In the fall of 2002 he did play in their pre-season games, but was let go and sent back to the Rangers for his fourth, and final, year.

This was a good turning event for Roy. As one of the best players on the Rangers he saw a lot of ice, allowing him to hone a lot of skills. He drew penalties and dove for the puck, wheeled and shifted around the ice with confidence. The Kitchener Rangers went on to win the Memorial Cup and, as the captain of the team, Roy excelled. Before Christmas of that year, he was tallying over two points a game and playing in every situation. Often, he carried the puck, and one of his best moves was cutting straight to the middle. Roy won the Stafford Smythe Memorial Trophy that year as Memorial Cup MVP.

He took this confidence to the Sabres training camp in the fall and when he was sent to the AHL he gritted his teeth and played like he had in Juniors. He scored a point per game, got noticed, and was called up to play most of the season with the Sabres. During the lockout, he again played in the AHL, and afterwards, in 2005-06, he didn't quite make the grade with the Sabres. He was sent to the AHL one more time. After scoring 20 points in just eight games in the AHL, the Sabres brought him back up to be in their lineup. Two hat tricks at the end of the season, and a good 2006 playoff run, made Roy an official Buffalo Sabre. He has continued to produce for the Sabres since.

The Hockey Canada scouts watched Roy over the years develop into a feisty, multi-dimensional player, but were most impressed by him when he played for the IIHF Men's World Championship Team in 2008 and in 2009. Both of those years, the teams won silver medals. The year where he saw such success with the Rangers, his last year of Juniors in 2003, Roy was also a member of the IIHF World Junior Team that won silver. That's three silver medals for Roy, and he's looking for gold.

Roy is smart, and he fairs well with good players. He has also established himself as the guy who can kill penalties.

Buffalo Sabres

Camp Highlights

During the orientation camp, Derek Roy showed that he was slippery and swift. He also had great versatility. For the Red and White game, he was winger on a line with Toews and St. Louis.

Getting ready to take a faceoff at the 2009 IIHF Men's World Championship in Switzerland.

Year	Team	Event	GP	G	A	PTS	PIM	Result
		Statistics– International						
		Regional						
2000	ONT	WU17	5	3	5	8	6	Silver
		National						
2000	CAN	SU18	3	0	2	2	4	Gold
2003	CAN	WJC	6	1	2	3	4	Silver
2008	CAN	WHC	9	5	5	10	6	Silver
2009	CAN	WHC	9	4	4	8	4	Silver
	CAN	INTL TOTAL	27	10	13	23	18	
	CAN	SR TOTAL	18	9	9	18	10	

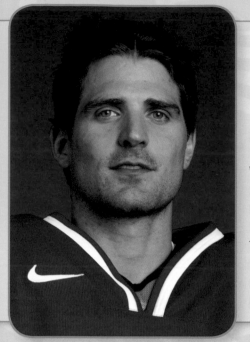

PATRICK SHARP

FORWARD #10

Shoots : Right
Height: 6'1"
Weight: 197 lbs
Birthdate: December 27, 1981
Birthplace: Winnipeg, MB.
Hometown: Thunder Bay, Ont.
Team: Chicago Blackhawks (NHL)
MHA: Thunder Bay MHA
NHL Draft: Philadelphia Flyers: 2001 (3, 95)
Last Amateur Club: University of Vermont (ECAC)

CANADA

There are players who when the coach tells them they want them, do so without a word. They don't care where they play, they just want to play. Patrick Sharp is a player who can move up and down the line and be used in any situation, all the while energizing his linemates. Although he's played centre most of his career, he can also switch gears and play wing. He's the kind of player who continues to work hard no matter the situation.

As well as having a good attitude, and being an all-around player, Sharp has developed some specialty skills. He's great on the penalty kill and he is also good along the boards when he is playing wing.

Sharp took the long route to the NHL. Growing up in Thunder Bay, Ontario he played for the Thunder Bay Flyers of the United States Hockey League for two years before he headed off to the Unites States to play for the University of Vermont. Drafted in 2001 to the Philadelphia Flyers going in the third round ninety-fifth overall, Sharp didn't make the transition to the NHL right away and spent the next season back at the University of Vermont. He still had a lot to learn, and his game needed much improvement before he was to become an NHL player. That year he was named the University of Vermont's MVP.

Doing the typical up and down route between the NHL and the AHL, Sharp played with the Flyers and their affiliate AHL team, the Philadelphia Phantoms for a few years. In his first year he was named the Phantom's Rookie of the Year. Sharp has always viewed his time in the AHL as positive, because in the 2004-05 season he was a member of the Calder Cup winning Phantoms. To win the

Image provided by his mother, Ruthann Sharp

Here is Patrick Sharp when he played for the Thunder Bay Elks AA at the age of 11. He played minor hockey with the Thunder Bay Minor Hockey Association.

Pets:
basset hound named Dudley

Favourite TV show:
Entourage

Something you migh not know:
Father is from Scotland

Favourite player to play against:
Steve Yzerman

2009 August orientation camp

Patrick Sharp

Calder Cup was a great experience for Sharp, and in every game he just kept trying to improve.

After a brief stint with the Flyers in 2005-06, Sharp was traded to the Chicago Blackhawks. He has been with the 'Hawks ever since, and at the age of 28, he is one of the "old" guys on an extremely young team.

At the beginning of his time with Chicago, his stats were average, and he just kept plugging away, trying to sort out his role, and trying to figure out where he fit in. Steady and sure, he played wherever the coach wanted him to play.

At the beginning of 2007, there was a definite shift in his overall game and he started to produce some stats. In 80 games he scored 20 goals and 15 assists.

Continuing his steady climb upwards, in 2007-08, Sharp once again made some significant jumps in his stats. At the end of the regular season, he had earned career highs in everything. On the record sheets he had scored 36 goals, 26 assists and 62 points, plus, he led the Blackhawks in power play goals (nine), shorthanded goals (seven), and game-winning goals (seven).

Rewarded for his production, Sharp signed a four-year contract extension with the Blackhawks in January of 2008, and on October 8, 2008, he was named an alternate captain along with Duncan Keith.

Because of his longer road to the top, Sharp has only played on one Canadian team. It was after his 2007 breakout season. In 2008, he played in the IIHF Men's World Championship in Quebec City/Halifax, winning a silver medal.

Sharp has what it takes to make this team because he can be that third or fourth line guy who, if given the chance, will deliver. Well-liked by everyone, he could just be that specialty team guy that Canada needs.

Skating hard at the 2008 IIHF Men's World Championship in Quebec/Halifax.

CANADA

Camp Highlights

Patrick Sharp played for Team White and was on a line with Smyth and Lecavalier. He proved he was a versatile player who doesn't make a lot of mistakes. In other words, he has the trustworthiness the management team is looking for.

Chicago Blackhawks

Statistics– International								
Year	Team	Event	GP	G	A	PTS	PIM	Result
		Regional						
		Not applicable						
		National						
2008	CAN	WHC	9	3	0	3	4	Silver
	CAN	INTL TOTAL	9	3	0	3	4	Silver
	CAN	SR TOTAL	9	3	0	3	4	

Patrick Sharp

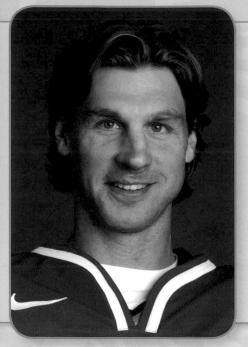

RYAN SMYTH

FORWARD #94

Shoots: **Left**
Height: **6'1"**
Weight: **190 lbs**
Birthdate: **February 21, 1976**
Birthplace: **Banff, Alta.**
Hometown: **Banff, Alta.**
Team: **Los Angeles Kings (NHL)**
MHA: **Banff MHA**
NHL Draft: **Edmonton Oilers: 1994 (1, 6)**
Last Amateur Club: **Moose Jaw Warriors (WHL)**

An icon on the Team Canada bench, Ryan Smyth deserved to be on this roster because of his history with international hockey and his tireless hard work to represent Canada. One of the comments made about Ryan from the Team Canada management, was that he, "always starts at the back of the bus but moves to the front."

They call him Captain Canada. Of all the players on this roster, Smyth has the most international experience, and has captained the most teams. In total, he has played on 11 Hockey Canada teams in 11 years, winning a total of four gold medals, one World Cup, and was named captain of the World Championship Canadian Team from 2001-2005. Every time he has donned the red and white jersey, he has played with pride and power, and he "knows what he represents."

Smyth is a player who totally understands his limitations, so he always plays to his strengths. He's smart that way. Probably his best strengths are his grittiness and toughness. For a slight guy, (he's 6'1" and only 190 lbs), he's powerful and he uses his power to his advantage to be feisty along the boards. He is a player who never backs down, never gives up on the puck, and just keeps digging and digging. He always puts the game first, and will take a hit to make a play, or take a puck to the mouth, and come back minutes later stitched up, ready to rejoin his line. And, of course, every coach he has played for knows that he is determined and goes to the net hard, playing both ends of the ice well.

In 1995, he started his international Hockey Canada career when he played in the IIHF World Junior Championship, bringing home the first of his gold medals. From there he went on to play in

A young Ryan Smyth in 1995 when he played for the IIHF World Junior Championship Team. The tournament took place in Red Deer, and Canada won the gold medal.

Image provided by Hockey Canada

Hockey hero:
Wayne Gretzky

Favourite activities outside of hockey:
skiing, poker

Favourite TV show:
Desperate Housewives

If not a hockey player would be a:
pro golfer

Person who had most influence on
hockey career growing up:
parents

Favourite band:
Nickelback

Favourite team growing up:
Edmonton Oilers

2009 August orientation camp

Ryan Smyth

CANADA

four straight Men's World Championships (1999- 2002), none of which produced gold. Prior to the World Championships in 2002, Smyth boarded the plane with the best of the best to travel to Salt Lake City with the coveted 2002 Men's Olympic Team. This was his first foray into the Olympic Games and his only Olympic gold medal to date. Definitely something to be proud of.

Smyth's international career continued and he played in two more World Championships (2003, 2004), picking up two more gold medals. His World Cup victory came when he was named to the 2004 World Cup Team, a team that was difficult to make. Only the best were on that roster. Smyth rounded off his international career with a silver medal in 2005 and a dismal performance at the 2006 Winter Olympics. He has not been a part of a Canadian team since 2006.

For over a decade, Smyth was the steady guy with the Edmonton Oilers, a fan favourite, an alternate captain, a gritty centre. In a tearful goodbye, in 2007, after 11 seasons, Smyth bade his team, and his home, farewell before he headed to New York to play for the Islanders. Since his departure, Smyth has been bounced around. From the Islanders, where he played just two months until he became an unrestricted free agent, he went to the Colorado Avalanche franchise for two years. Just this summer, Smyth was once again traded, this time to the Los Angeles Kings.

As far as Smyth's future on this 2010 Olympic squad, much will depend on how he fares with the Kings this fall. Will he find some players who he gels with, who he can work with, who can help him earn points? In the big scheme, he will have to play to his strengths, but that is something he definitely knows how to do. Ryan Smyth knows how to make it to the front of the bus on time.

Camp Highlights
Named the first star of the night in the Calgary Herald for the Red and White Scrimmage, Captain Canada proved he was still a contender for the team. He opened the scoring in the second period of the game with an unassisted goal on Martin Brodeur. And he also set up the second Team White goal. He was a "grinding presence."

Los Angeles Kings

A feisty Ryan Smyth looking to score a goal at the 2006 Olympics in Turin, Italy.

		Statistics– **International**						
Year	Team	Event	GP	G	A	PTS	PIM	Result
		Regional						
1994	PAC	U17	-	-	-	-	-	
		National						
1995	CAN	WJC	7	2	5	7	4	Gold
1999	CAN	WHC	10	0	2	2	12	4th
2000	CAN	WHC	9	3	6	9	0	4th
2001	CAN	WHC	7	2	3	5	2	5th
2002	CAN	OLY	6	0	1	1	0	Gold
2002	CAN	WHC	7	4	0	4	2	6th
2003	CAN	WHC	9	2	2	4	2	Gold
2004	CAN	WHC	9	2	2	4	2	Gold
2004	CAN	WCH	6	3	1	4	2	1st
2005	CAN	WHC	9	2	1	3	6	Silver
2006	CAN	OLY	6	0	1	1	4	7th
	CAN	INTL TOTAL	85	20	24	44	36	
	CAN	SR TOTAL	59	15	16	31	26	

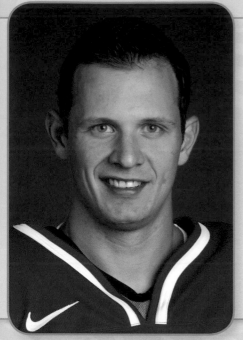

JASON SPEZZA

FORWARD #19

Shoots: **Right**
Height: **6'3"**
Weight: **214 lbs**
Birthdate: **June 13, 1983**
Birthplace: **Weston, Ont.**
Hometown: **Mississauga, Ont.**
Team: **Ottawa Senators (NHL)**
MHA: **Greater Toronto Hockey League (GTHL)**
NHL Draft: **Ottawa Senators: 2001 (1, 2)**
Last Amateur Club: **Belleville Bulls (OHL)**

A late addition to the roster, Jason Spezza was invited to the 2010 Canadian Olympic orientation camp at the end of July, nearly a month after the original roster was announced. Ryan Getzlaf informed Hockey Canada that he couldn't make the camp due to his injury, and the next best on the wait list was Spezza. Executive Director, Steve Yzerman, made the call to Spezza and, naturally, he was excited. When he had been left off the initial roster, Spezza had been determined to play well enough in the fall to be granted another look. But attending camp is the better deal, and Spezza knows that it gives him a leg up on the competition. The Hockey Canada management team knows that this is great news for Spezza but they also know that "he has a lot of guys to climb over if he is to make the team."

With that said, they also know that with this kind of team, and with Spezza's known determination, anything can happen.

Spezza is a likeable guy and a good offensive forward. It was unfortunate that his NHL team, the Ottawa Senators, had such a poor year in 2008-09. The Senators had a run for the cup in 2006-07, and that is when Spezza was on top of his game.

Spezza is talented and was always good as a teenager. Often those "good" qualities come with practice, and in his teens, he spent a lot of time working, training, and honing his skills. From all his practice, he made himself into a player with good hands, great passing, skills and the ability to see the ice very well.

Spezza is one of the few players on this roster who actually began his Junior career underage, at 15. Starting off in the OHL with the Brampton Battalion in 1998-99, he was the youngest on his team,

A young Jason Spezza with Steve Yzerman when Yzerman was still a player. Jason was thrilled to get this photo.

2009 August orientation camp

Nickname:
Spezz

Something you might not know:
appeared in a Minute Maid commercial at the age of five

Favourite sport other than hockey:
lacrosse

Hockey hero:
Mario Lemieux

Favourite NHL team growing up:
Toronto Maple Leafs

Youth hockey accomplishments:
named Athlete of the Year by the City of Mississauga in 1999

Jason Spezza

but he still managed to scrape together 71 points, including 22 goals and 49 assists. After his year with the Battalion, he had to go into the Priority Draft and he ended up on the expansion team, the Mississauga Ice Dogs. In 52 games, he earned 61 points. But his experience with this new OHL franchise ended in the early part of the 2000-01 season, and he found himself suiting up with the Windsor Spitfires. Obviously, this was a good move for Spezza because he ended up with an OHL career high of 116 points in 66 games.

This was definite fuel for the 2001 NHL Entry Draft and Spezza went in the first round, second overall to the Ottawa Senators, just behind Ilya Kovalchuk who went to the Atlanta Thrashers.

The following year, the Senators liked what they saw in Spezza at their training camp but in the end they sent him back to the OHL. Throughout his last OHL year, Spezza was traded one last time to the Belleville Bulls, and when their season ended, Spezza had come third in the OHL for scoring with 115 points. He was assigned to the Senators farm team in the AHL. Spezza finished off with 11 points in 11 games.

That summer, Spezza knew he had to do something that would help him crack the Senators roster, so he hired a personal trainer and skating coach, plus he went on a strict diet to lose weight. Even with all his extra work, Spezza played the up and down game before he played his first full year season in the NHL in 2003-04.

For the Hockey Canada management team, Spezza's reputation in international hockey has really helped him earn this spot on the roster. Spezza played for three consecutive years with the Canadian World Junior Team. Selected to the team in 2000, he became one of the few 16 year olds to make the team, but that year, he did spend most of his time on the bench.

He didn't give up and the following year, he once again made the team, but this time he logged a lot of time, earning the title of tournament All-Star. That year, Spezza showed what he was

Ottawa Senators

made of, and when he went head-to-head with Russian player, Ilya Kovalchuk, he totally dominated. In his third year with the World Junior Team, in 2002, Spezza played with Heatley, and they were a force. They enjoyed playing together, even though Spezza didn't score as many goals as he would have liked.

Spezza's international career didn't stop after Juniors. He has also been on two Men's World Championship Teams (2008, 2009) and he was named an alternate for the 2006 Olympic Team. In total, for Canada, he has won two bronze medals and three silver medals.

Can he play in the pressure filled gold-medal games? That is yet to be determined. It is also yet to be determined how he will show during the fall of the 2009-10 season. Spezza has a chance, just like everyone else.

Camp Highlights

Spezza centred a Team White line and initially he started off with Eric Staal and Corey Perry. With one man out (Gagne), Spezza moved around and played with different wingers. All in all, he had a decent camp and certainly is on the list for a reason.

2009 August orientation camp

Statistics– International								
Year	Team	Event	GP	G	A	PTS	PIM	Result
Regional								
Not applicable								
National								
1998-99	CAN	NATS	7	0	2	2	2	-
1999-00	CAN	NATS	-	-	-	-	-	-
2000	CAN	WJC	7	0	2	2	2	Bronze
2001	CAN	WJC	7	3	3	6	2	Bronze
2002	CAN	WJC	7	0	4	4	8	Silver
2008	CAN	WHC	9	1	2	3	0	Silver
2009	CAN	WHC	9	7	4	11	2	Silver
	CAN	INTL TOTAL	46	11	17	28	16	
	CAN	SR TOTAL	25	8	8	16	4	

MARTIN ST. LOUIS

FORWARD #26

Shoots: **Left**
Height: **5'9"**
Weight: **177 lbs**
Birthdate: **June 18, 1975**
Birthplace: **Laval, QC**
Hometown: **Laval, QC**
Team: **Tampa Bay Lightning (NHL)**
MHA: **Laval MHA**
NHL Draft: **Undrafted**
Last Amateur Club: **University of Vermont (ECAC)**

Everyone knows Martin St. Louis. He is the little guy, the one who minor hockey coaches refer to when they have a keen, skilled, young player who is small but wants desperately to make it big. They say, "Martin St. Louis did it, he made it, you can too."

But the fact remains that there aren't many Martin St. Louis' in the world of hockey, that small player (5'9", 177 lbs), who plays like he's big. St. Louis is special. A strong competitor, he can play with anybody and against anybody. He can play at a very high pace. The Hockey Canada management team has watched St. Louis over the years, and knows that he, "always plays well in big games." St. Louis doesn't get rattled easily, and will pay the price over and over to make the play. He gives hits and takes hits; he doesn't care who he is up against, he'll play them. Mentally tough, he doesn't let his size hinder him from being a top player; in fact, he doesn't think his size should come into play at all.

So, in the Hockey Canada minds, it is a given that he would be put on this roster. In fact, because of how he deals with his career, they don't look at him as a small player anymore, just a strong, dangerous, and experienced one.

As a teenager, with a big dream—a dream that many tried to squash because of his size—St. Louis decided to take the College–Hockey route. His school of choice was the University of Vermont. The list of awards he earned in four years of playing for the University of Vermont Catamounts is staggering. It seems to go on forever, like a roll of credits after a movie. He made rookie teams, All-Star teams, and was named player of the year. At the

Martin St. Louis played for four years with the University of Vermont Catamounts.

Tampa Bay Lightning

Hockey hero:
Mats Naslund

Favourite movie:
Forrest Gump

Favourite activities outside
hockey:
**playing/spending time with
my kids**

If not a hockey player would be:
try to be an athlete

Most exciting part of hosting
Games in Canada:
**playing in front of home
fans**

Person who had most influence on
career growing up:
Dad

Best concert ever attended:
U2

Favourite food:
ice cream

Martin St. Louis

Sitting on the bench waiting for his shift at the 2009 IIHF Men's World Championship in Switzerland.

NCAA Championships, he was named to the All-Tournament Team. For three years running he was a finalist for the Hobey-Baker Award for College Player of the Year.

Even with all of these accomplishments to his name, when his draft year rolled around, he went unnoticed. Perhaps a bit of a slap in the face. St. Louis didn't let this defeat his dream, but rather made him that much more determined, so he signed with the Cleveland Lumberjacks of the International Hockey League. This league went belly-up in 2001, and wasn't exactly the breeding ground for scouts trying to seek out players for the NHL. St. Louis darted around the ice anyway and during the IHL playoffs, Bill Barber, a former Flyer noticed him and made a mental note about the little guy. He was also noticed by the Calgary Flames, and they gave him a free-agent deal, assigning him to the Saint John Flames of the AHL.

St. Louis jumped at the chance to be one step closer to the NHL. The move to the AHL proved good for him and he settled in to do his time, never losing sight of his long-range goal. For three years, he played hard and became the Saint John's top scorer. The Calgary Flames coaches watched him, liking what they saw. He was fast and had grit and maybe, they thought, he could be used as a fore-checker and penalty killer.

So they called him up and put him on the fourth line. The role proved tough on St. Louis and after 13 games he was sent back to Saint John, where he settled in and once again performed well.

The next season, he got the call again to head to Calgary and this time he played better, or so he thought. The Flames staff didn't exactly agree with St. Louis and didn't offer him a new contract but Tampa Bay decided to pick him up on a two-year contract.

St. Louis he has been with the Lightning for eight years now and has emerged as one of their best players. His road to the top has been long and varied, but he remained tough and strong on and off the ice. In 2004 St. Louis was a huge contributor to the Lightning when they won the Stanley Cup. That year he also won the Hart Trophy.

St. Louis has done some time on the Hockey Canada bench and knows how to play internationally. He's won two silver medals at IIHF Men's World Championships, (2008, 2009), played in one Olympic Games, (2006) and played on the 2004 World Cup Team that won the Cup.

Everybody likes St. Louis; coaches like his energy and commitment to the game and players enjoy his spirit and toughness. He blasts around the ice every shift, creating openings and scoring opportunities. He is one determined hockey player.

2009 August orientation camp

Camp Highlights
Martin St. Louis proved he more than deserved to be at the camp. He played for Team White and when he replaced Jarome Iglina on the Crosby/Nash line, he looked fast and skilled. All in all, this line had some of the chemistry that Team Canada is looking for.

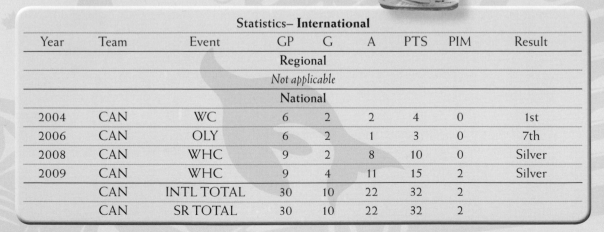

Statistics– International								
Year	Team	Event	GP	G	A	PTS	PIM	Result
Regional								
Not applicable								
National								
2004	CAN	WC	6	2	2	4	0	1st
2006	CAN	OLY	6	2	1	3	0	7th
2008	CAN	WHC	9	2	8	10	0	Silver
2009	CAN	WHC	9	4	11	15	2	Silver
	CAN	INTL TOTAL	30	10	22	32	2	
	CAN	SR TOTAL	30	10	22	32	2	

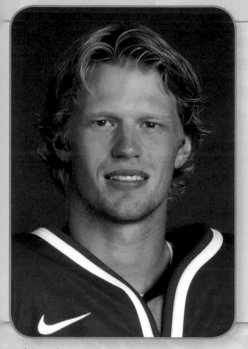

ERIC STAAL

FORWARD #12

Shoots: **Left**
Height: **6'4"**
Weight: **205 lbs**
Birthdate: **October 29, 1984**
Birthplace: **Thunder Bay, Ont.**
Hometown: **Thunder Bay, Ont.**
Team: **Carolina Hurricanes (NHL)**
MHA: **Thunder Bay MHA**
NHL Draft: **Carolina Hurricanes: 2003 (1, 2)**
Last Amateur Club: **Peterborough Petes (OHL)**

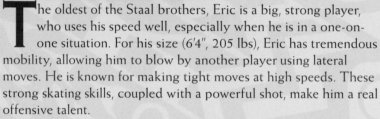

CANADA

The oldest of the Staal brothers, Eric is a big, strong player, who uses his speed well, especially when he is in a one-on-one situation. For his size (6'4", 205 lbs), Eric has tremendous mobility, allowing him to blow by another player using lateral moves. He is known for making tight moves at high speeds. These strong skating skills, coupled with a powerful shot, make him a real offensive talent.

According to the Hockey Canada management team, Eric emerged as a star player right from the day he laced up his skates to play in the NHL. He was young too, extremely young, when he went right from playing with the Peterborough Petes in the OHL to the NHL, with no stops in between. His transition was flawless.

In his last year of Junior Hockey with the Petes, Eric scored 39 goals for 98 points in just 66 games. He was named to the OHL second All-Star Team and the CHL first All-Star Team that year. Then, he was chosen to play in the 2003 CHL/NHL Top Prospects game. When the Draft rolled around, Eric sat in the stands awaiting his fate. Rumours were flying about who would go first and his name had been bantered around. Eric didn't go first, but second, to the Carolina Hurricanes, behind Marc-André Fleury, another member of the orientation-camp roster.

In the fall, right after being drafted, Eric said goodbye to his family before heading south to Carolina. He made the Hurricanes' roster at their training camp, and, thus his NHL career began. As a rookie, he scored 11 goals, and 20 assists for 31 points, which was enough to give him a shot at playing in the Young Stars game during the NHL All-Star week.

Image provided by his mother, Linda Staal

A young Eric Staal learning how to stand on his skates. He played most of his minor hockey career with the Thunder Bay MHA.

Home Ice

2009 August orientation camp

Hockey hero:
Wayne Gretzky, Joe Sakic

Favourite movie:
The Hangover

Favourite activity outside of hockey:
fishing

If not a hockey player would be a:
sod farmer

Favourite song on mp3 player:
**Tonight's Going to
be a Good Night—
Black Eyed Peas**

Favourite book:
**Lone Survivor by Marcus
Luttrell**

Favourite road city:
Vancouver

First job:
**working on his parents'
sod farm**

Eric Staal

CANADA

The next season was the lockout of 2004-05 and being young, fresh, and eager to continue getting better at the game, Eric played for the Lowell Lock Monsters of the AHL, where he played 77 games and earned 77 points.

Back in the NHL for the 2005-06 season, Eric had a huge breakout year when he reached the 100 mark for points in the season. This was also the season that the Hurricanes went on to win the Stanley Cup Championship. Leading the Hurricanes, Eric managed to collect 28 points during the playoffs, which was the highest amount for his team. This terrific showing during the playoffs and the regular season helped him to be fourth in the voting for the Hart Trophy.

That successful showing in such a recent Stanley Cup Final has helped to solidify Eric as a threat. He also went the distance when he played for Canada at two IIHF Men's World Championships. In 2007, Eric travelled to Moscow and the team won a gold medal and in 2008, he played for the Men's World Team in Quebec/Halifax, winning silver. He was named as an alternate for the 2006 Olympic team but didn't actually play any games. Eric played for Canada in the 2002 IIHF Under-18 championship. Because of his strong and early entrance to the NHL in 2003, Eric didn't have the chance to play on any of Canada's World Junior Teams, simply because the Hurricanes needed him to play over the Christmas period.

Over the years, Eric has racked up many awards and made many All-Star teams, including the 2007, 2008 and 2009 NHL All-Star Teams. One of the most memorable awards he received was when he played in the 2008 NHL All-Star Game, and won the MVP. Eric is definitely a skilled hockey player and a strong contender to make the 2010 Canadian Olympic squad. Most are curious as to which Staal brother(s) will make this team. Let's wait and see.

Carolina Hurricanes

Camp Highlights

Eric played wing for Team White, and was on a line with winger Corey Perry and centre Jason Spezza. A highlight for Eric was in the shootout when he cleverly snuck the puck by Steve Mason.

Eric is not happy with the call. This was taken at the 2007 IIHF World Championship in Russia.

		Statistics– **International**						
Year	Team	Event	GP	G	A	PTS	PIM	Result
		Regional						
2001	ONT	WU17	--	--	--	--	--	Bronze
		National						
2001	CAN	SU18	5	0	0	0	7	Gold
2002	CAN	WU18	8	2	5	7	4	6th
2007	CAN	WHC	9	5	5	10	6	Gold
2008	CAN	WHC	8	4	3	7	6	Silver
	CAN	INTL TOTAL	8	4	3	7	6	
	CAN	SR TOTAL	30	11	13	24	23	

Eric Staal

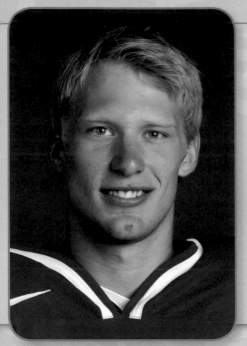

JORDAN STAAL

FORWARD #11

Shoots: **Left**
Height: **6'4"**
Weight: **217 lbs**
Birthdate: **September 10, 1988**
Birthplace: **Thunder Bay, Ont.**
Hometown: **Thunder Bay, Ont.**
Team: **Pittsburgh Penguins (NHL)**
MHA: **Thunder Bay MHA**
NHL Draft: **Pittsburgh Penguins: 2006 (1, 2)**
Last Amateur Club: **Peterborough Petes (OHL)**

Eric is the eldest Staal brother on this roster, and Jordan is the youngest. Not only is he the youngest brother to make the list, but he is still considered young in the world of hockey. With a birthday of September 10, 1988, he will be just 21 years old at Olympic time.

There is quite a difference in playing styles between the two brothers in the forward category. Over the years, Jordan has been known as a checking centreman, and he played it well. Big and strong, he played an extremely physical game, and was always eager to use his body to get the puck without taking a lot of penalties. In his last year of Junior, in 2005-06, he scored 28 goals and 40 assists for 68 points, which is good but not fantastic. That wasn't his style of game. His game was to play a strong two-way game.

When he hit the NHL though, he showed signs of changing his style, learning how to play a more offensive game. He started to emerge as a complete player, someone who could also play the puck and pick up points. The Hockey Canada management team saw great potential in Jordan Staal. Jordan was a key player for the Pittsburgh Penguins in 2008-09, and was instrumental in their Stanley Cup victory. The Hockey Canada scouts watched him closely and liked that he had developed into a player who was now an entire package.

Jordan played in the OHL for just two years before he was drafted in the 2006 NHL Entry Draft by the Pittsburgh Penguins, going, like his brother Eric, second overall behind Eric Johnson. His Draft year coincided with his brother Eric playing in the Stanley Cup finals so June was an exciting month for the Staal family.

Image provided by his mother, Linda Staal

It's hard to believe Jordan Staal was once that small. Like his brothers, he played most of his minor hockey career with the Thunder Bay MHA.

Idol:
Tiger Woods

Favourite TV show:
Family Guy

Favourite activity outside hockey:
fishing

If not a hockey player would be a:
sod farmer

Person who had most influence on
hockey career growing up:
Dad

Favourite singer:
Keith Urban

Hockey hero:
Wayne Gretzky

Favourite book:
**Lone Survivor by
Marcus Luttrell**

2009 August orientation camp

Jordan Staal

CANADA

It was no surprise to anyone, that when he showed up to training camp in the fall of 2006, he made the Penguins roster. That year, he played in 81 of their 82 games, giving him a full rookie season under his belt. The first time on the ice with big brother Eric brought about some sibling banter.

Jordan's rookie season didn't go unnoticed because he managed to pick up a fistful of records. He became the youngest player to score in a penalty shot; the first player since 1982 to score his first three career goals short-handed; he was the youngest player to record a hat trick; and he set an NHL rookie record scoring seven short-handed goals. When he scored his first hat trick, the Penguins were playing the Toronto Maple Leafs in Toronto. This was a big moment for Jordan, because he grew up watching the Leafs on television.

That spring, Jordan was also nominated for the Calder Memorial Trophy for Rookie of the Year. He didn't win but just being in the category with such great players like Evgeni Malkin and Paul Stastny was a huge boost for him. He also made the NHL All-Rookie Team in 2007.

The next season, Jordan started off slow and his production tapered off from his rookie year. Nonetheless, he was still a driving force as one of the young up-and-coming players in the league, and he still put forth a valiant effort as Pittsburgh made a run for the Cup.

The big year for Jordan came in 2009 when Pittsburgh won the Stanley Cup, and he was definitely one of their key players. Offensively, he was back on track and during the regular season, he recorded over 20 points more than the previous season, evening out at a 48-point total. In the Penguins 24 playoff games, he secured only four goals and five assists, but he was a main ingredient for the team's win. That's when the Hockey Canada staff said, "We want this kid on our August Orientation-Camp roster."

Will he be the Staal brother who makes it? Will his brothers join him?

2009 August orientation camp

Camp Highlights
Jordan Staal was the lone Staal brother on Team Red in the intersquad game. Playing against his brothers, he wasn't afraid to go to the puck, or to carry it into the zone, or make some fancy moves to get around his opposition. He picked up a penalty for holding in the third period.

Pittsburgh Penguins

Statistics– **International**								
Year	Team	Event	GP	G	A	PTS	PIM	Result
Regional								
2005	ONT	WU17	--	--	--	--	--	4th
National								
2005	CAN	SU18	5	1	1	2	12	Gold
2007	CAN	WHC	9	0	2	2	0	Gold
	CAN	INTL TOTAL	14	1	3	4	12	
	CAN	SR TOTAL	9	0	2	2	0	

Jordan Staal

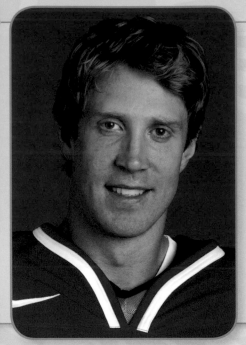

JOE THORNTON

FORWARD #19

Shoots: **Left**
Height: **6'4"**
Weight: **235 lbs**
Birthdate: **July 2, 1979**
Birthplace: **London, Ont.**
Hometown: **St. Thomas, Ont.**
Team: **San Jose Sharks (NHL)**
MHA: **St. Thomas MHA**
NHL Draft: **Boston Bruins: 1997 (1, 1)**
Last Amateur Club: **Sault Ste. Marie Greyhounds (OHL)**

CANADA

He's internationally savvy, having played international hockey on five teams. Joe Thornton is a big guy, (6'4" and 235 lbs) with hands that are like fluffy down pillows, soft and pliable. He uses those soft hands in the offensive zone to slip the puck over to his teammates or to fly it by the goaltenders himself. But his hands are the only thing about Joe Thornton that is soft. The rest of his play is extremely powerful and strong.

The Hockey Canada management team knows that Thornton is a guy who is a "quiet leader." They know that he is dependable and trustworthy, and are looking at him to emerge as an elite player if he makes the team. They also expect him to dominate physically because of his size. In the round-table discussions, management compared Joe Thornton to Ryan Getzlaf. But they also made a note that "he plays well with Heatley and Nash."

At the age of 16, Joe was 6'4" and weighed in at 200 lbs. Yes, he was big, making his leap to the OHL a pleasant experience. For two years he played for the Sault Ste. Marie Greyhounds, and in his rookie year, he dominated the pack with 30 goals and 46 assists to earn the OHL Rookie of the Year award. Scouts began taking note of his name, and in his second year, they stood along the boards with pens and paper detailing Joe's every move. That second year, Thornton stole the show, averaging at least two points a game, and sending off perfect passes to his teammates. By the end of the season, he was being dubbed as the best player the OHL had produced in years and rightly so because he recorded 41 goals, 81 assists for a grand total of 122 points.

Here is Joe Thornton winning a trophy with the Southwest, Ontario Team.

Favourite movie:
The Last Samurai

Favourite TV shows:
24 and Prison Break

Favourite NHL team growing up:
Los Angeles Kings

Hockey hero:
Pat Lafontaine

If not a hockey player would be a:
pilot

If he could meet anyone
it would be:
Alexander the Great

Three wishes:
**health, happiness and
world peace**

Favourite activity outside hockey:
golf

San Jose Sharks

Joe Thornton

189

CANADA

2009 August
orientation camp

Funnily enough, Joe was not named to the First OHL First All-Star Team that year. Of course, that was just a little hiccup, because when June rolled around and it was time for the 1997 NHL Entry Draft, the first name that was called was Joe Thornton's. Stepping on the stage, he slipped the Boston Bruins jersey over his head.

The media waited for Thornton to show up in Boston, as they all wanted to know about this new phenomenon, this new "Eric Lindros." Was he going to perform? Be a superstar?

That first year, Thornton didn't become a superstar, and instead, played mostly fourth line duties, seeing little ice, if any, in the last minutes of play. For some reason, he never really got on track that year. He had terrible stats and the hockey media loved to talk trash about the big, young kid but that didn't matter to the Bruins. Thornton played another six years with the Bruins, working his way up the lines, until he was playing that first-line roll he was used to in Juniors.

It took time for him to find his groove in the NHL. With his success in the OHL and going number one in the Draft, no one anticipated that it was going to take that much time, but his real breakout year came in 2001-02. The Bruins coaches had found a good combination for Thornton with Sergei Samsonov, and together, this duo performed. Early in the season, Thornton was racing ahead in an effort to win the NHL scoring title, then he was injured and the dream of winning the Art Ross Trophy ended. Also, that year his name was left off the 2002 Olympic Team. He was named as an alternative.

During the lockout, in 2004-05, Thornton went to Switzerland where he played for Davos, and also played at Christmas in the Spengler Cup, which the home-team Davos won. When his year in Europe ended, and he returned to Canada, Thornton started back again with the Bruins. But on November 30, 2005, Thornton was traded to the San Jose Sharks in a huge four-player deal.

Sometimes trades happen for a reason. Playing in San Jose worked out great for Thornton and he easily adapted, soon becoming an alternate captain for the team.

Thornton has picked up his fair share of awards and trophies along his hockey journey, and he has also graced the Hockey Canada bench five times, winning a gold medal (1997 IIHF World Junior), a World Cup (2004 World Cup), and a silver medal (2005 IIHF World Championship). In 2005, in Austria at the IIHF Men's World Championship, Thornton was named the MVP and to the tournament All-Star Team.

After being left off the 2002 Olympic roster, Thornton was named to the 2006 Olympic team so he is yet another player that will be looking for redemption in 2010. Thornton has yet to win that coveted Olympic gold medal.

Camp Highlights

In the Red and White game, Joe Thornton started out on a line playing centre between Patrick Marleau and Dany Heatley. The lines switched as the game went on and Thornton took all this in stride and used his strengths to play with everyone he was matched up with.

2009 August orientation camp

Statistics– International

Year	Team	Event	GP	G	A	PTS	PIM	Result
		Regional						
1995	ONT	WU17	--	--	--	--	--	Gold
		National						
1996	CAN	SU18	5	4	5	9	14	Gold
1997	CAN	WJC	7	2	2	4	0	Gold
2001	CAN	WHC	6	1	1	2	6	5th
2004	CAN	WC	6	1	5	6	0	1st
2005	CAN	WHC	9	6	10	16	4	Silver
2006	CAN	OLY	6	1	2	3	0	7th
	CAN	INTL TOTAL	39	15	25	40	24	
	CAN	SR TOTAL	27	9	18	27	10	

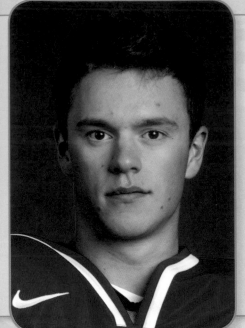

JONATHAN TOEWS

FORWARD #19

Shoots: **Left**
Height: **6'2"**
Weight : **209 lbs**
Birthdate: **April 29, 1988**
Birthplace: **Winnipeg, Man.**
Hometown: **Winnipeg, Man.**
Team: **Chicago Blackhawks (NHL)**
MHA: **Winnipeg MHA**
NHL Draft: **Chicago Blackhawks: 2006 (1, 3)**
Last Amateur Club: **University of North Dakota (WCHA)**

CANADA

Another member of the new breed of young player is Jonathan Toews. He is highly skilled, powerful, and a true character guy. Toews is known to have the most incredible leg strength, which gives him unprecedented ability to find openings.

This knack to get to the openings, coupled with his great hands, and great vision on the ice, makes him a powerful forward. No matter what zone he is in, he works and uses his body to make plays, especially along the boards and down low. The Hockey Canada management team thinks he is "just so strong." Plus, they like the fact that he is an ultra competitor, someone who will go to the wall every game, shift, and stride.

In his teens, Toews could have easily followed the Junior route after being drafted first overall by the Tri-City Americans in the Bantam draft, but he chose to play College Hockey. This is not the ordinary route that most top players choose, as most NHL scouts are scouring the CHL games. He knew his first year of College was also his NHL Draft year, and he also knew it would be tougher for him to get noticed. But Toews made his decision to go to College and stuck with it—for two years anyway.

Earning a full-ride scholarship to the University of North Dakota, he fast became one of their best players, helping his team, the Fighting Sioux, make it to the Frozen Four. His stats were good in his rookie year, and he proved to be a powerful threat. Months prior to his playoff stint at the Frozen Four, Toews suited up for Canada and played at the IIHF World Junior Championship, winning a gold medal.

In June, at the NHL Entry Draft, even though Toews hadn't followed the Junior route, he was drafted third overall to the

Here is Jonathan with a big "C" on his jersey when he played minor hockey with the Winnipeg Minor Hockey Association.

Image provided by Pat Brisson and Judd Moldaver

2009 August orientation camp

Hockey hero:
Joe Sakic

Favourite activity outside of hockey:
relaxing with friends

If not a hockey player would be a:
baseball player

Person who had most influence on
hockey career growing up:
parents

Favourite band:
Our Lady Peace

Favourite team growing up:
Los Angeles Kings

Favourite magazine:
Maxim

Favourite book:
**Lone Survivor
by Marcus Luttrell**

Jonathan Toews

Chicago Blackhawks. When the fall rolled around, after a summer of heavy training, Toews went back to College.

Once again, Hockey Canada named him to their 2007 Canadian Junior Team roster and he ended up being named the Top Forward for the tournament, becoming a fan favourite as well. He scored three shootout goals in a semifinal victory against the United States. This appearance on the world stage gave Toews huge recognition. Canadian fans were glued to their televisions during the Christmas holidays, and he became the kid to watch.

That spring, North Dakota once more made it to the Frozen Four and Toews was a contributing factor to the team's success. It was also in the spring of 2007, that Toews answered the call to play for Team Canada at the Men's World Championships. When the team won the gold medal, Toews became the first Canadian player ever to win gold at the IIHF World Junior Championships and at the IIHF World Championship in just one season. He accomplished this while still in his teens.

Finally, Toews decided that he did want to play in the NHL, and after two years of College he made his way to Chicago. The Blackhawks were a perfect team for him, because they were so young, fresh, and eager. Toews climbed right into the driver's seat and started performing, and by the end of the season, despite a few injuries along the way, he was nominated for the Calder Cup Trophy.

For a young player, Toews is mature and wise, and he was rewarded for his maturity on July 18, when he was named team captain for the Blackhawks, becoming the third youngest team captain in NHL history. Preceding him are Sidney Crosby and Vincent Lecavalier—both members of this prestigious roster.

Jonathan Toews is a player to watch and a player who has every right to be on the 2010 Canadian Olympic Team.

Chicago Blackhawks

Camp Highlights

Overall, Jonathan Toews did really well at the camp. In the Red and White game, he was on Team White and started off playing centre between Derek Roy and Martin St. Louis. Partway through the game, Jarome Iginla took Martin St. Louis' place on the line and Toews played with Iginla. Like every player on the this roster, Toews will be looked at in the fall.

Toews has been a strong player for Team Canada. Here he is looking for a pass at the 2007 IIHF Men's World Championships in Russia. Canada won the gold medal.

Year	Team	Event	GP	G	A	PTS	PIM	Result
Statistics– International								
Regional								
2004	WST	WU17	6	8	4	12	2	Gold
National								
2005	CAN	SU18	5	5	4	9	0	Gold
2006	CAN	WJC	6	0	2	2	2	Gold
2007	CAN	WJC	6	4	3	7	12	Gold
2007	CAN	WHC	9	2	5	7	6	Gold
2008	CAN	WHC	9	2	3	5	8	Silver
	CAN	INTL TOTAL	35	13	17	30	28	
	CAN	SR TOTAL	18	4	8	12	14	

STATISTICS–JUNIOR & PROFESSIONAL

GOALIES

MARTIN BRODEUR

Statistics– Club Team			Regular Season								Playoffs							
Season	Team	League	GP	MIN	GA	SO	AVG	W-L-T-OTL	SOG	Sv%	GP	MIN	GA	SO	AVG	W-L	SOG	Sv%
1989-90	STH	QMJHL	42	2333	156	0	4.01	22-13-2	1252	0.875	12	678	46	0	4.07	5-7	381	0.879
1990-91	STH	QMJHL	25	2946	162	2	3.30	22-24-4	1414	0.885	4	232	16	0	4.14	0-4	113	0.858
1991-92	STH	QMJHL	48	2846	161	3	3.39	27-16-4	1523	0.888	5	317	14	0	2.65	2-3	201	0.930
1991-92	NJ	NHL	4	179	10	0	3.35	2-1-0	85	0.882	1	32	3	0	5.63	0-1	15	0.800
1992-93	UTI	AHL	32	1952	131	2	4.03	14-13-5	1002	0.884	4	258	18	0	4.19	1-3	?	
1993-94	NJ	NHL	47	2625	105	3	2.40	27-11-8	1238	0.915	17	1171	38	1	1.95	8-9	531	0.928
1994-95	NJ	NHL	40	2184	89	3	2.45	19-11-8	908	0.902	20	1222	34	3	1.67	16-4	463	0.927
1995-96	NJ	NHL	77	4433	173	6	2.34	34-30-12	1954	0.911	-	-	-	-	-	-	-	-
1996-97	NJ	NHL	67	3838	120	10	1.88	37-14-13	1633	0.927	10	659	19	2	1.73	5-5	268	0.929
1997-98	NJ	NHL	70	4128	130	10	1.89	43-17-8	1569	0.917	7	366	12	0	1.97	2-4	164	0.927
1998-99	NJ	NHL	70	4239	162	4	2.29	39-21-10	1728	0.906	7	425	20	0	2.82	3-4	139	0.856
1999-00	NJ	NHL	72	4312	161	6	2.24	43-20-8	1797	0.910	23	1450	39	2	1.61	16-7	537	0.927
2000-01	NJ	NHL	72	4297	166	9	2.32	42-17-11	1762	0.906	25	150	52	4	2.07	15-10	507	0.897
2001-02	NJ	NHL	73	4347	156	4	2.15	38-26-9	1655	0.906	6	381	9	1	1.42	2-4	145	0.938
2002-03	NJ	NHL	73	4374	147	9	2.02	41-23-9	1706	0.914	24	1491	41	7	1.65	16-8	622	0.934
2003-04	NJ	NHL	75	4555	154	11	2.03	38-26-9	1845	0.917	5	298	13	0	2.62	1-4	133	0.902
2005-06	NJ	NHL	73	4365	187	5	2.57	43-23-0-7	2105	0.911	9	533	20	1	2.25	5-4	261	0.923
2006-07	NJ	NHL	78	4697	171	12	2.18	48-23-0-7	2182	0.922	11	688	28	1	2.44	5-6	332	0.916
2007-08	NJ	NHL	77	4635	168	4	2.17	44-27-0-6	2089	0.920	5	301	16	0	3.19	1-4	147	0.891
2008-09	NJ	NHL	31	1814	73	5	2.41	19-9-0-3	870	0.916	7	427	17	1	2.39	3-4	239	0.929
NHL CAREER			999	59022	2172	101	2.21	557-299-105-23	25126	0.914	101	10949	361	23	1.98	98-78	4503	0.920

MARC-ANDRÉ FLEURY

Statistics– Club Team			Regular Season								Playoffs							
Season	Team	League	GP	MIN	GA	SO	AVG	W-L-T-OTL	SOG	Sv%	GP	MIN	GA	SO	AVG	W-L	SOG	Sv%
2000-01	C.B.	QMJHL	35	1705	115	0	4.05	12-13-0-2	1006	0.886	2	32	4	0	7.50	0-1	21	0.810
2001-02	C.B.	QMJHL	55	3043	141	2	2.78	26-14-0-8	1662	0.915	16	1003	55	0	3.29	9-7	548	0.900
2002-03	C.B.	QMJHL	51	2889	162	2	3.36	17-24-0-6	1801	0.910	4	228	4	0	4.47	0-4	178	0.904
2003-04	PIT	NHL	21	1154	70	1	3.64	4-14-0-2	675	0.896	-	-	-	-	-	-	-	-
2003-04	C.B.	QMJHL	10	606	20	0	1.98	8-1-0-1	297	0.933	4	251	13	0	3.11	1-3	114	0.886
2004-05	W-B	AHL	54	3029	127	5	2.52	26-19-0-4	1286	0.901	4	151	11	0	4.37	0-2	70	0.886
2005-06	W-B	AHL	12	727	19	0	1.57	10-2-0-0	312	0.939	5	311	18	0	3.47	2-3	154	0.883
2006-07	PIT	NHL	67	3905	184	5	2.83	40-16-0-9	1954	0.906	5	287	18	0	3.76	1-4	150	0.880
2007-08	W-B	AHL	5	297	7	0	1.41	3-2-0-0	140	0.950	-	-	-	-	-	-	-	-
2007-08	PIT	NHL	35	1857	72	4	2.33	19-10-0-2	909	0.921	20	1251	41	3	1.97	14-6	610	0.933
2008-09	PIT	NHL	62	3641	162	4	2.67	35-18-0-7	1850	0.912	24	1447	63	0	2.61	16-8	686	0.908
NHL CAREER			235	13366	640	15	2.87	111-85-0-26	6873	0.907	49	2985	122	3	2.45	31-18	1446	0.916

Roberto Luongo

Statistics– Club Team			Regular Season								Playoffs							
Season	Team	League	GP	MIN	GA	SO	AVG	W-L-T-OTL	SOG	Sv%	GP	MIN	GA	SO	AVG	W-L	SOG	Sv%
1995-96	VD	QMJHL	23	1201	74	0	3.70	6-11-0-4	608	0.878	3	68	5	0	4.41	0-1	37	0.865
1996-97	VD	QMJHL	60	3305	171	2	3.10	32-22-0-2	1742	0.902	13	777	44	0	3.40	8-5	460	0.904
1997-98	VD	QMJHL	54	3046	157	7	3.09	27-20-0-5	1704	0.908	17	1019	37	2	2.18	14-3	555	0.933
1997-98	VD	MemCup	-	-	-	-	-	-	-	-	3	180	19	0	6.33	0-3	n/a	n/a
1998-99	BATH	QMJHL	52	2517	163	1	3.60	20-17-3-0	1495	0.899	23	1400	64	0	2.74	16-6	756	0.915
1998-99	BATH	MemCup	-	-	-	-	-	-	-	-	3	180	11	0	3.67	0-3	n/a	n/a
1999-00	LOW	AHL	26	1517	74	3.31	0	10-12-0-4	807	0.908	6	359	18	0	3.01	3-3	222	0.909
1999-00	NYI	NHL	24	1292	70	3.25	1	7-14-0-1	730	0.904	-	-	-	-	-	-	-	-
2000-01	LOU	AHL	3	178	10	0	3.37	1-2-0-0	121	0.917	-	-	-	-	-	-	-	-
2000-01	FLA	NHL	47	2628	107	5	2.44	12-24-0-7	1333	0.920	-	-	-	-	-	-	-	-
2001-02	FLA	NHL	58	3030	140	4	2.77	16-33-0-4	1653	0.915	-	-	-	-	-	-	-	-
2002-03	FLA	NHL	65	3627	164	6	2.71	20-34-0-7	2011	0.918	-	-	-	-	-	-	-	-
2003-04	FLA	NHL	72	4252	172	7	2.43	25-33-0-14	2475	0.931	-	-	-	-	-	-	-	-
2005-06	FLA	NHL	75	4305	213	4	2.97	35-30-0-9	2488	0.914	-	-	-	-	-	-	-	-
2006-07	VAN	NHL	76	4490	171	5	2.29	47-22-0-6	2169	0.921	12	847	25	0	1.77	5-7	427	0.941
2007-08	VAN	NHL	73	4233	168	6	2.38	35-29-0-9	2029	0.917	-	-	-	-	-	-	-	-
2008-09	VAN	NHL	54	3181	124	9	2.34	33-13-0-7	1542	0.920	10	618	26	1	2.52	6-4	304	0.914
	NHL CAREER		544	31038	1329	47	2.57	230-232-0-64	16430	0.919	22	1465	51	1	2.09	11-11	731	0.930

Steve Mason

Statistics– Club Team			Regular Season								Playoffs							
Season	Team	League	GP	MIN	GA	SO	AVG	W-L-T-OTL	SOG	Sv%	GP	MIN	GA	SO	AVG	W-L	SOG	Sv%
2005-06	LDN	OHL	12	497	22	0	2.66	5-3-0-0	321	0.931	4	150	7	0	2.80	0-1	79	0.911
2006-07	LDN	OHL	62	3733	199	2	3.20	45-13-0-4	2123	0.914	16	931	54	0	3.48	9-7	635	0.915
2007-08	KIT	OHL	42	2530	106	3	2.51	32-7-0-3	1263	0.916	5	313	10	1	1.92	5-0	175	0.943
2008-09	SYR	AHL	3	184	5	0	1.63	2-1	74	0.932	-	-	-	-	-	-	-	-
2008-09	CBJ	NHL	61	3664	140	10	2.29	33-20-0-7	1658	0.916	4	239	17	0	4.27	0-4	139	0.878
	NHL CAREER		61	3664	140	10	2.29	33-20-0-7	1658	0.916	4	239	17	0	4.27	0-4	139	0.878

Cam Ward

Statistics– Club Team			Regular Season								Playoffs							
Season	Team	League	GP	MIN	GA	SO	AVG	W-L-T-OTL	SOG	Sv%	GP	MIN	GA	SO	AVG	W-L	SOG	Sv%
2000-01	R.D.	WHL	1	60	1	0	0.00	1-0-0-0			-	-	-	-	-	-	-	-
2001-02	R.D.	WHL	46	2694	102	1	2.27	30-11-0-4	1145	0.911	23	1502	53	2	2.12	14-9	662	0.920
2002-03	R.D.	WHL	57	3368	118	5	2.10	40-13-0-3	1474	0.920	23	1407	49	3	2.09	14-9	607	0.919
2003-04	R.D.	WHL	56	3338	114	4	2.05	31-16-0-8	1550	0.926	19	1200	37	3	1.85	10-9	637	0.945
2004-05	LOW	AHL	50	2829	94	6	1.99	27-17-0-3	1487	0.937	11	664	28	2	2.53	5-6	312	0.918
2005-06	LOW	AHL	2	118	5	0	2.54	0-2-0-0	59	0.915	-	-	-	-	-	-	-	-
2005-06	CAR	NHL	28	1484	91	0	3.68	14-8-0-2	682	0.882	23	1320	47	2	2.14	15-8	584	0.920
2006-07	CAR	NHL	60	3422	167	2	2.93	30-21-0-6	1725	0.897	-	-	-	-	-	-	-	-
2007-08	CAR	NHL	69	3930	180	4	2.75	37-25-0-5	1870	0.904	-	-	-	-	-	-	-	-
2008-09	CAR	NHL	68	3928	160	6	2.44	39-23-0-5	1901	0.916	18	1101	49	2	2.67	8-10	576	0.915
	NHL CAREER		225	12764	598	12	2.81	120-77-0-18	6169	0.903	41	2421	96	4	2.38	23-18	1160	0.917

DEFENCEMEN

FRANCOIS BEAUCHEMIN

Statistics– Club Team			Regular Season					Playoffs				
Season	Team	League	GP	G	A	PTS	PIM	GP	G	A	PTS	PIM
1996-97	LAV	QMJHL	66	7	21	28	132	3	0	0	0	2
1997-98	LAV	QMJHL	70	12	35	47	132	16	1	3	4	23
1998-99	BATH	QMJHL	31	4	17	21	53	23	2	16	18	55
1998-99	BATH	MemCup	-	-	-	-	-					
1999-00	MNC	QMJHL	71	19	67	86	99	16	2	11	13	14
2000-01	QUE	AHL	56	3	6	9	44	-	-	-	-	-
2001-02	QUE	AHL	56	8	11	19	88	3	0	1	1	0
2001-02	MISS	ECHL	7	1	3	4	2	-	-	-	-	-
2002-03	HAM	AHL	75	7	21	28	92	23	1	9	10	16
2002-03	MTL	NHL	1	0	0	0	0	-	-	-	-	-
2003-04	HAM	AHL	77	9	27	36	57	10	2	4	6	18
2004-05	SYR	AHL	72	3	27	30	55	-	-	-	-	-
2005-06	ANA	NHL	72	8	28	36	52	16	3	6	9	11
2006-07	ANA	NHL	71	7	21	28	49	20	4	4	8	16
2007-08	ANA	NHL	82	2	19	21	59	6	0	0	0	26
2008-09	ANA	NHL	20	1	4	5	12	13	1	0	1	15
NHL CAREER			246	21	59	90	172	55	8	10	18	68

JAY BOUWMEESTER

Statistics– Club Team			Regular Season					Playoffs				
Season	Team	League	GP	G	A	PTS	PIM	GP	G	A	PTS	PIM
1998-99	M.H.	WHL	8	2	1	3	2	-	-	-	-	-
1999-00	M.H.	WHL	64	13	21	34	26	-	-	-	-	-
2000-01	M.H.	WHL	61	14	39	53	44	-	-	-	-	-
2001-02	M.H.	WHL	61	11	50	61	42	-	-	-	-	-
2002-03	FLA	NHL	82	4	12	16	14	-	-	-	-	-
2002-03	S.A.	AHL	2	0	1	1	2	-	-	-	-	-
2003-04	FLA	NHL	61	2	18	20	30	-	-	-	-	-
2004-05	CHI	AHL	82	10	16	26	62	18	0	0	0	14
2005-06	FLA	NHL	82	5	41	46	79	-	-	-	-	-
2006-07	FLA	NHL	82	12	30	42	66	-	-	-	-	-
2007-08	FLA	NHL	82	15	22	37	68	-	-	-	-	-
2008-09	FLA	NHL	82	15	27	42	68	-	-	-	-	-
NHL CAREER			471	53	150	203	329	0	0	0	0	0

DAN BOYLE

Statistics– Club Team

Season	Team	League	Regular Season					Playoffs				
			GP	G	A	PTS	PIM	GP	G	A	PTS	PIM
1997-98	CIN	AHL	8	0	3	3	20	5	0	1	1	4
1998-99	FLA	NHL	22	3	5	8	6	-	-	-	-	-
1998-99	KENT	AHL	53	8	34	42	87	12	3	5	8	16
1999-00	LOU	AHL	58	14	38	52	75	4	0	2	2	8
1999-00	FLA	NHL	13	0	3	3	4	-	-	-	-	-
2000-01	LOU	AHL	6	0	5	5	12	-	-	-	-	-
2000-01	FLA	NHL	69	4	18	22	28	-	-	-	-	-
2001-02	TB	NHL	66	8	18	26	39	-	-	-	-	-
2002-03	TB	NHL	77	13	40	53	44	11	0	7	7	6
2003-04	TB	NHL	78	9	30	39	60	23	2	8	10	16
2004-05	DJUR	SEL	32	9	9	18	47	12	2	3	5	26
2005-06	TB	NHL	79	15	38	53	38	5	1	3	4	6
2006-07	TB	NHL	82	20	43	63	62	6	0	1	1	2
2007-08	TB	NHL	37	4	21	25	57	-	-	-	-	-
2008-09	SJ	NHL	77	16	41	57	52	6	2	2	4	8
NHL CAREER			600	92	257	349	390	51	5	21	26	38

BRENT BURNS

Statistics– Club Team

Season	Team	League	Regular Season					Playoffs				
			GP	G	A	PTS	PIM	GP	G	A	PTS	PIM
2002-03	BRM	OHL	86	15	25	40	14	11	5	6	11	6
2003-04	MIN	NHL	36	1	5	6	12	-	-	-	-	-
2003-04	HOU	AHL	1	0	1	1	2	-	-	-	-	-
2004-05	HOU	AHL	73	11	16	27	57	5	0	0	0	4
2005-06	MIN	NHL	72	4	12	16	32	-	-	-	-	-
2006-07	MIN	NHL	77	7	18	25	26	5	0	1	1	14
2007-08	MIN	NHL	82	15	28	43	80	6	0	2	2	6
2008-09	MIN	NHL	59	8	19	27	45	-	-	-	-	-
NHL CAREER			326	35	82	117	195	11	0	3	3	20

DREW DOUGHTY

Statistics– Club Team

Season	Team	League	Regular Season					Playoffs				
			GP	G	A	PTS	PIM	GP	G	A	PTS	PIM
2005-06	GUE	OHL	65	5	28	33	40	14	0	13	13	18
2006-07	GUE	OHL	67	21	53	74	76	4	2	3	5	8
2007-08	GUE	OHL	58	13	37	50	68	10	3	6	9	14
2008-09	LA	NHL	81	6	21	27	56	-	-	-	-	-
NHL CAREER			71	6	21	27	56	0	0	0	0	0

MIKE GREEN

Statistics– Club Team			Regular Season					Playoffs				
Season	Team	League	GP	G	A	PTS	PIM	GP	G	A	PTS	PIM
2000-01	SAS	WHL	7	0	2	2	0	7	0	1	1	2
2001-02	SAS	WHL	62	3	20	23	57	6	0	2	2	6
2002-03	SAS	WHL	72	6	36	42	70	4	0	0	0	6
2003-04	SAS	WHL	59	14	25	39	92	-	-	-	-	-
2004-05	SAS	WHL	67	14	52	66	105	4	0	0	0	6
2005-06	HER	AHL	56	9	34	43	79	21	3	15	18	30
2005-06	WSH	NHL	22	1	2	3	18	-	-	-	-	-
2006-07	WSH	NHL	70	2	10	12	36	-	-	-	-	-
2007-08	WSH	NHL	82	18	38	56	62	7	3	4	7	15
2008-09	WSH	NHL	68	31	42	73	68	14	1	8	9	12
NHL CAREER			242	52	92	144	184	21	4	12	16	27

DAN HAMHUIS

Statistics– Club Team			Regular Season					Playoffs				
Season	Team	League	GP	G	A	PTS	PIM	GP	G	A	PTS	PIM
1998-99	P.G.	WHL	56	1	3	4	45	7	1	2	3	8
1999-00	P.G.	WHL	70	10	23	33	140	13	2	3	5	35
2000-01	P.G.	WHL	62	13	47	60	125	6	2	3	5	15
2001-02	P.G.	WHL	59	10	50	60	135	7	0	5	5	16
2002-03	MIL	AHL	68	6	21	27	81	6	0	3	3	2
2003-04	NSH	NHL	80	7	19	26	57	6	0	2	2	6
2004-05	MIL	AHL	76	13	38	51	85	7	0	2	2	10
2005-06	NSH	NHL	82	7	31	38	70	5	0	2	2	2
2006-07	NSH	NHL	82	6	14	20	66	5	0	1	1	2
2007-08	NSH	NHL	72	3	23	26	67	6	1	1	2	6
2008-09	NSH	NHL	82	3	23	26	67	-	-	-	-	-
NHL CAREER			405	27	110	137	326	22	1	6	7	16

DUNCAN KEITH

Statistics– Club Team			Regular Season					Playoffs				
Season	Team	League	GP	G	A	PTS	PIM	GP	G	A	PTS	PIM
2001-02	MICH	CCHA	41	3	12	15	18					
2002-03	MICH	CCHA	15	3	6	9	8					
2002-03	KEL	WHL	37	11	35	46	60	19	3	11	14	12
2003-04	NOR	AHL	75	7	18	25	44	8	1	1	2	6
2004-05	NOR	AHL	79	9	17	26	78	6	0	0	0	14
2005-06	CHI	NHL	81	9	12	21	79	-	-	-	-	-
2006-07	CHI	NHL	82	2	29	31	76	-	-	-	-	-
2007-08	CHI	NHL	82	12	20	32	56	-	-	-	-	-
2008-09	CHI	NHL	77	8	36	44	60	17	0	6	6	10
NHL CAREER			322	31	97	128	271	17	0	6	6	10

SCOTT NIEDERMAYER

Statistics– Club Team			Regular Season					Playoffs				
Season	Team	League	GP	G	A	PTS	PIM	GP	G	A	PTS	PIM
1989-90	KAM	WHL	64	14	55	69	64	17	2	14	16	35
1989-90	KAM	MemCup	-	-	-	-	-	3	1	1	2	2
1990-91	KAM	WHL	57	26	56	82	52					
1991-92	NJ	NHL	4	0	1	1	2	-	-	-	-	-
1991-92	KAM	WHL	35	7	32	39	61	17	9	14	23	28
1991-92	KAM	MemCup	-	-	-	-	-	5	2	5	7	6
1992-93	NJ	NHL	80	11	29	40	47	5	0	3	3	2
1993-94	NJ	NHL	81	10	36	46	42	20	2	2	4	8
1994-95	NJ	NHL	48	4	15	19	18	20	4	7	11	10
1995-96	NJ	NHL	79	8	25	33	46	-	-	-	-	-
1996-97	NJ	NHL	81	5	30	35	64	10	2	4	6	6
1997-98	NJ	NHL	81	14	43	57	27	6	0	2	2	4
1998-99	UTAH	IHL	5	0	2	2	0	-	-	-	-	-
1998-99	NJ	NHL	72	11	35	46	26	7	1	3	4	18
1999-00	NJ	NHL	71	7	31	38	48	22	5	2	7	10
2000-01	NJ	NHL	57	6	29	35	22	21	0	6	6	14
2001-02	NJ	NHL	76	11	22	33	30	6	0	2	2	6
2002-03	NJ	NHL	81	11	28	39	62	24	2	16	18	16
2003-04	NJ	NHL	81	14	40	54	44	5	1	0	1	6
2005-06	ANA	NHL	82	13	50	63	96	16	2	9	11	14
2006-07	ANA	NHL	79	15	54	69	86	21	3	8	11	26
2007-08	ANA	NHL	48	8	17	25	16	6	0	2	2	4
2008-09	ANA	NHL	82	14	45	59	70	13	3	7	10	11
NHL CAREER			1183	162	530	692	746	202	25	73	98	155

DION PHANEUF

Statistics– Club Team			Regular Season					Playoffs				
Season	Team	League	GP	G	A	PTS	PIM	GP	G	A	PTS	PIM
2001-02	R.D.	WHL	67	5	12	17	170	21	0	2	2	14
2002-03	R.D.	WHL	71	16	14	30	185	23	7	7	14	34
2003-04	R.D.	WHL	62	19	24	43	126	19	2	9	11	30
2004-05	R.D.	WHL	55	24	32	56	73	7	1	4	5	12
2005-06	CGY	NHL	82	20	29	49	93	7	1	0	1	7
2006-07	CGY	NHL	79	17	33	50	98	6	1	0	1	7
2007-08	CGY	NHL	82	17	43	60	182	7	3	4	7	4
2008-09	CGY	NHL	80	11	36	47	100	5	0	3	3	4
NHL CAREER			323	65	141	206	473	25	5	7	12	22

CHRIS PRONGER

Statistics– Club Team

Season	Team	League	Regular Season					Playoffs				
			GP	G	A	PTS	PIM	GP	G	A	PTS	PIM
1991-92	PBO	OHL	63	17	45	62	90	10	1	8	9	28
1992-93	PBO	OHL	61	15	62	77	108	21	15	25	40	51
1992-93	PBO	MemCup	-	-	-	-	-	5	1	5	6	8
1993-94	HFD	NHL	81	5	25	30	113	-	-	-	-	-
1994-95	HFD	NHL	43	5	9	14	54	-	-	-	-	-
1995-96	STL	NHL	78	7	18	25	110	13	1	5	6	16
1996-97	STL	NHL	79	11	24	35	143	6	1	1	2	22
1997-98	STL	NHL	81	9	27	36	180	10	1	9	10	26
1998-99	STL	NHL	67	13	33	46	113	13	1	4	5	28
1999-00	STL	NHL	79	14	48	62	92	7	3	4	7	32
2000-01	STL	NHL	51	8	39	47	75	15	1	7	8	32
2001-02	STL	NHL	78	7	40	47	120	9	1	7	8	24
2002-03	STL	NHL	5	1	3	4	10	7	1	3	4	14
2003-04	STL	NHL	80	14	40	54	88	5	0	1	1	16
2005-06	EDM	NHL	80	12	44	56	74	24	5	16	21	26
2006-07	ANA	NHL	66	13	46	59	69	19	3	12	15	26
2007-08	ANA	NHL	72	12	31	43	128	6	2	3	5	12
2008-09	ANA	NHL	82	11	37	48	88	13	2	8	10	12
NHL CAREER			1022	142	464	606	1457	147	22	80	102	286

ROBYN REGEHR

Statistics– Club Team

Season	Team	League	Regular Season					Playoffs				
			GP	G	A	PTS	PIM	GP	G	A	PTS	PIM
1996-97	KAM	WHL	64	4	19	23	96	5	0	1	1	18
1997-98	KAM	WHL	65	4	10	14	120	5	0	3	3	8
1998-99	KAM	WHL	54	12	20	32	130	12	1	4	5	21
1999-00	STJ	AHL	5	0	0	0	0	-	-	-	-	-
1999-00	CGY	NHL	57	5	7	12	46	-	-	-	-	-
2000-01	CGY	NHL	71	1	3	4	70	-	-	-	-	-
2001-02	CGY	NHL	77	2	6	8	93	-	-	-	-	-
2002-03	CGY	NHL	76	0	12	12	87	-	-	-	-	-
2003-04	CGY	NHL	82	4	14	18	74	26	2	7	9	20
2005-06	CGY	NHL	68	6	20	26	67	7	1	3	4	6
2006-07	CGY	NHL	78	2	19	21	75	1	0	0	0	0
2007-08	CGY	NHL	82	5	15	20	79	7	0	2	2	2
2008-09	CGY	NHL	75	0	8	8	73	0	0	0	0	0
NHL CAREER			666	25	104	129	664	41	3	12	15	28

STEPHANE ROBIDAS

Statistics– Club Team			Regular Season					Playoffs				
Season	Team	League	GP	G	A	PTS	PIM	GP	G	A	PTS	PIM
1993-94	SHAW	QMJHL	67	3	18	21	33	1	0	0	0	0
1994-95	SHAW	QMJHL	71	13	56	69	44	15	7	12	19	4
1995-96	SHAW	QMJHL	67	23	56	79	54	6	1	5	6	10
1996-97	SHAW	QMJHL	67	24	51	75	59	7	4	6	10	14
1997-98	FRE	AHL	79	10	21	31	50	4	0	2	2	0
1998-99	FRE	AHL	79	8	33	41	59	15	1	5	6	10
1999-00	QUE	AHL	76	14	31	45	36	3	0	1	1	0
1999-00	MTL	NHL	1	0	0	0	0					
2000-01	MTL	NHL	65	6	6	12	14					
2001-02	MTL	NHL	56	1	10	11	14	2	0	0	0	4
2002-03	DAL	NHL	76	3	7	10	35	12	0	1	1	20
2003-04	CHI	NHL	59	3	10	13	41	-	-	-	-	-
2004-05	FRA	DEL	51	15	32	47	64	6	1	2	3	6
2005-06	DAL	NHL	75	5	15	20	67	5	0	2	2	4
2006-07	DAL	NHL	75	0	17	17	86	7	0	1	1	2
2007-08	DAL	NHL	82	9	17	26	85	18	3	8	11	12
2008-09	DAL	NHL	72	3	23	26	76	-	-	-	-	-
NHL CAREER			561	30	105	135	418	44	3	12	15	42

BRENT SEABROOK

Statistics– Club Team			Regular Season					Playoffs				
Season	Team	League	GP	G	A	PTS	PIM	GP	G	A	PTS	PIM
2000-01	LETH	WHL	4	0	0	0	0	-	-	-	-	-
2001-02	LETH	WHL	67	6	33	39	70	4	1	1	2	2
2002-03	LETH	WHL	69	9	33	42	113	-	-	-	-	-
2003-04	LETH	WHL	61	12	29	41	107	-	-	-	-	-
2004-05	LETH	WHL	63	12	42	54	107	5	1	2	3	10
2004-05	NOR	AHL	3	0	0	0	2	6	0	1	1	6
2005-06	CHI	NHL	69	5	27	32	60	-	-	-	-	-
2006-07	CHI	NHL	81	4	20	24	104	-	-	-	-	-
2007-08	CHI	NHL	82	9	23	32	90	-	-	-	-	-
2008-09	CHI	NHL	82	8	18	26	62	17	1	11	12	14
NHL CAREER			314	26	88	114	316	17	1	11	12	14

MARC STAAL

Statistics– Club Team			Regular Season					Playoffs				
Season	Team	League	GP	G	A	PTS	PIM	GP	G	A	PTS	PIM
2003-04	SBY	OHL	61	1	13	14	34	7	1	2	3	4
2004-05	SBY	OHL	65	6	20	26	53	12	0	4	4	15
2005-06	SBY	OHL	57	11	38	49	60	10	0	8	8	8
2005-06	HFD	AHL	-	-	-	-	-	12	0	2	2	8
2006-07	SBY	OHL	53	5	29	34	68	21	5	15	20	22
2007-08	NYR	NHL	80	2	8	10	42	10	1	2	3	8
2008-09	NYR	NHL	82	3	12	15	64	7	1	0	1	0
NHL CAREER			162	5	20	25	106	17	2	2	4	8

SHEA WEBER

Statistics– Club Team			Regular Season					Playoffs				
Season	Team	League	GP	G	A	PTS	PIM	GP	G	A	PTS	PIM
2001-02	KEL	WHL	5	0	0	0	0	-	-	-	-	-
2002-03	KEL	WHL	70	2	16	18	167	19	1	4	5	26
2003-04	KEL	WHL	60	12	20	32	126	17	3	14	17	16
2003-04	KEL	MemCup	-	-	-	-	-	4	1	3	4	4
2004-05	KEL	WHL	55	12	29	41	95	18	9	8	17	25
2004-05	KEL	MemCup	-	-	-	-	-	3	0	3	3	4
2005-06	MIL	AHL	46	12	15	27	49	14	6	5	11	16
2005-06	NSH	NHL	28	2	10	12	42	4	2	0	2	8
2006-07	NSH	NHL	79	17	23	40	60	5	0	3	3	2
2007-08	NSH	NHL	54	6	14	20	49	6	1	3	4	0
2008-09	NSH	NHL	81	23	30	53	80	-	-	-	-	-
NHL CAREER			242	48	75	123	231	15	3	6	9	16

FORWARDS

JEFF CARTER

Statistics– Club Team			Regular Season					Playoffs				
Season	Team	League	GP	G	A	PTS	PIM	GP	G	A	PTS	PIM
2001-02	SSM	OHL	63	18	17	35	12	4	0	0	0	2
2002-03	SSM	OHL	61	35	36	71	55	4	0	2	2	2
2003-04	SSM	OHL	57	36	30	66	26	-	-	-	-	-
2003-04	PHA	AHL	-	-	-	-	-	12	4	1	5	0
2004-05	SSM	OHL	55	34	40	74	40	7	5	5	10	6
2004-05	PHA	AHL	-	-	-	-	-	21	12	11	23	12
2005-06	PHA	NHL	81	23	19	42	40	6	0	0	0	10
2006-07	PHA	NHL	62	14	23	37	48	-	-	-	-	-
2007-08	PHA	NHL	82	29	24	53	55	17	6	5	11	12
2008-09	PHA	NHL	82	46	38	84	68	6	1	0	1	8
NHL CAREER			307	112	104	216	211	29	7	5	12	30

DAN CLEARY

Statistics– Club Team			Regular Season					Playoffs				
Season	Team	League	GP	G	A	PTS	PIM	GP	G	A	PTS	PIM
1994-95	BEL	OHL	62	26	55	81	62	6	7	10	17	23
1995-96	BEL	OHL	64	64	62	115	74	14	10	17	27	40
1996-97	BEL	OHL	64	32	48	80	88	6	3	4	7	6
1997-98	CHI	NHL	6	0	0	0	0	-	-	-	-	-
1997-98	BEL	OHL	30	16	31	47	14	10	6	7	13	10
1997-98	IND	IHL	4	2	1	3	6	-	-	-	-	-
1998-99	CHI	NHL	35	4	5	9	24	-	-	-	-	-
1998-99	PORT	AHL	30	9	17	26	74	-	-	-	-	-
1998-99	HAM	AHL	9	0	1	1	7	3	0	0	0	0
1999-00	HAM	AHL	58	22	52	74	108	5	2	3	5	18
1999-00	EDM	NHL	17	3	2	5	8	4	0	1	1	2
2000-01	EDM	NHL	81	14	21	35	7	6	1	1	2	8
2001-02	EDM	NHL	65	10	19	28	51	-	-	-	-	-
2002-03	EDM	NHL	57	4	13	17	31	-	-	-	-	-
2003-04	PHX	NHL	68	6	11	17	42	-	-	-	-	-
2004-05	MORA	SEL	47	11	26	37	38	-	-	-	-	-
2005-06	DET	NHL	77	3	12	15	40	6	0	1	1	6
2006-07	DET	NHL	71	20	20	40	24	18	4	8	12	30
2007-08	DET	NHL	63	20	22	42	33	22	2	1	3	4
2008-09	DET	NHL	74	14	26	40	46	23	9	6	15	12
NHL CAREER			614	98	151	249	336	79	16	18	34	62

SIDNEY CROSBY

Statistics– Club Team			Regular Season					Playoffs				
Season	Team	League	GP	G	A	PTS	PIM	GP	G	A	PTS	PIM
2003-04	RIM	QMJHL	59	54	81	135	74	9	7	9	16	13
2004-05	RIM	QMJHL	62	66	102	168	84	13	14	17	31	16
2005-06	PIT	NHL	81	39	63	102	110	-	-	-	-	-
2006-07	PIT	NHL	79	36	84	120	60	5	3	2	5	4
2007-08	PIT	NHL	53	24	48	72	39	20	6	21	27	12
2008-09	PIT	NHL	77	33	70	103	76	24	15	16	31	14
NHL CAREER			290	132	265	397	285	49	24	39	63	30

SHANE DOAN

Statistics– Club Team

Season	Team	League	Regular Season					Playoffs				
			GP	G	A	PTS	PIM	GP	G	A	PTS	PIM
1992-93	KAM	WHL	51	7	12	19	65	13	0	1	1	8
1993-94	KAM	WHL	52	24	24	48	88	-	-	-	-	-
1994-95	KAM	WHL	71	37	57	94	106	21	6	10	16	16
1994-95	KAM	MemCup	-	-	-	-	-	4	4	5	9	6
1995-96	WPG	NHL	74	7	10	17	101	6	0	0	0	6
1996-97	PHX	NHL	63	4	8	12	49	4	0	0	0	2
1997-98	SPR	AHL	39	21	21	42	64	-	-	-	-	-
1997-98	PHX	NHL	33	5	6	11	46	6	1	0	1	6
1998-99	PHX	NHL	79	6	16	22	54	7	2	2	4	6
1999-00	PHX	NHL	81	26	25	51	66	4	1	2	3	8
2000-01	PHX	NHL	76	26	37	63	89	5	2	2	4	6
2001-02	PHX	NHL	81	20	29	49	61	-	-	-	-	-
2002-03	PHX	NHL	82	21	37	58	86	-	-	-	-	-
2003-04	PHX	NHL	79	27	41	68	47	-	-	-	-	-
2005-06	PHX	NHL	82	30	36	66	123	-	-	-	-	-
2006-07	PHX	NHL	73	27	28	55	73	-	-	-	-	-
2007-08	PHX	NHL	80	28	50	78	59	-	-	-	-	-
2008-09	PHX	NHL	82	31	42	73	72	-	-	-	-	-
NHL CAREER			965	258	365	623	915	32	6	6	12	34

SIMON GAGNE

Statistics– Club Team

Season	Team	League	Regular Season					Playoffs				
			GP	G	A	PTS	PIM	GP	G	A	PTS	PIM
1996-97	BEAU	QMJHL	51	9	22	31	49	-	-	-	-	-
1997-98	QUE	QMJHL	53	30	39	69	26	12	11	5	16	23
1998-99	QUE	QMJHL	61	50	70	120	42	13	9	8	17	4
1999-00	PHA	NHL	80	20	28	48	22	17	5	5	10	2
2000-01	PHA	NHL	69	27	32	59	18	6	3	0	3	0
2001-02	PHA	NHL	79	33	33	66	32	5	0	0	0	2
2002-03	PHA	NHL	46	9	18	27	16	13	4	1	5	6
2003-04	PHA	NHL	80	24	21	45	29	18	5	4	9	12
2005-06	PHA	NHL	72	47	32	79	38	6	3	1	4	4
2006-07	PHA	NHL	76	41	27	68	30	-	-	-	-	-
2007-08	PHA	NHL	25	7	11	18	4	-	-	-	-	-
2008-09	PHA	NHL	79	34	40	74	42	6	3	1	4	2
NHL CAREER			606	242	242	484	144	71	23	12	35	26

RYAN GETZLAF

Statistics– Club Team			Regular Season					Playoffs				
Season	Team	League	GP	G	A	PTS	PIM	GP	G	A	PTS	PIM
2001-02	CGY	WHL	63	9	9	18	34	7	2	1	3	4
2002-03	CGY	WHL	70	29	39	68	121	5	1	1	2	6
2003-04	CGY	WHL	49	28	47	75	97	7	5	1	6	12
2004-05	CGY	WHL	51	29	25	54	02	12	4	13	17	18
2004-05	PORT	AHL	-	-	-	-	-	10	1	4	5	4
2005-06	PORT	AHL	17	8	25	33	36	1	0	0	0	4
2005-06	ANA	NHL	57	14	25	39	22	16	3	4	7	13
2006-07	ANA	NHL	82	25	33	58	66	21	7	10	17	32
2007-08	ANA	NHL	77	24	58	82	94	6	2	3	5	6
2008-09	ANA	NHL	81	25	66	91	121	13	4	14	18	25
NHL CAREER			97	88	82	70	03	56	16	31	47	76

DANY HEATLEY

Statistics– Club Team			Regular Season					Playoffs				
Season	Team	League	GP	G	A	PTS	PIM	GP	G	A	PTS	PIM
1999-00	WISC	WCHA	38	28	28	56	32	unavailable				
2000-01	WISC	WCHA	39	24	33	57	74	unavailable				
2001-02	ATL	NHL	82	26	41	67	56	-	-	-	-	-
2002-03	ATL	NHL	77	41	48	89	58	-	-	-	-	-
2003-04	ATL	NHL	31	13	12	25	18	-	-	-	-	-
2004-05	BERN	SUI	16	14	10	24	58	-	-	-	-	-
2004-05	KAZ	RUS	11	3	1	3	22	-	-	-	-	-
2005-06	OTT	NHL	82	50	53	103	86	10	3	9	12	11
2006-07	OTT	NHL	82	50	55	105	74	20	7	15	22	14
2007-08	OTT	NHL	71	41	41	82	76	4	0	1	1	6
2008-09	OTT	NHL	82	39	33	72	88	-	-	-	-	-
NHL CAREER			507	260	283	543	456	34	10	25	35	31

JAROME IGINLA

Statistics– Club Team			Regular Season					Playoffs				
Season	Team	League	GP	G	A	PTS	PIM	GP	G	A	PTS	PIM
1993-94	KAM	WHL	48	6	23	29	33	19	3	6	9	10
1993-94	KAM	MemCup	-	-	-	-	-	4	0	2	2	4
1994-95	KAM	WHL	72	33	38	71	111	21	7	11	18	34
1994-95	KAM	MemCup	-	-	-	-	-	4	4	2	6	7
1995-96	KAM	WHL	63	63	73	136	120	16	16	13	29	44
1995-96	CGY	NHL	-	-	-	-	-	2	1	1	2	0
1996-97	CGY	NHL	82	21	29	50	37	-	-	-	-	-
1997-98	CGY	NHL	70	13	19	43	29	-	-	-	-	-
1998-99	CGY	NHL	82	28	23	51	58	-	-	-	-	-
1999-00	CGY	NHL	77	29	34	63	26	-	-	-	-	-
2000-01	CGY	NHL	77	31	40	71	62	-	-	-	-	-
2001-02	CGY	NHL	82	52	44	96	77	-	-	-	-	-
2002-03	CGY	NHL	75	35	32	67	49	-	-	-	-	-
2003-04	CGY	NHL	81	41	32	73	84	26	13	9	22	45
2005-06	CGY	NHL	82	35	32	67	86	7	5	3	8	11
2006-07	CGY	NHL	70	39	55	94	40	6	2	2	4	12
2007-08	CGY	NHL	82	50	48	98	83	7	4	5	9	2
2008-09	CGY	NHL	82	35	54	89	37	6	3	1	4	0
NHL CAREER			942	409	442	951	668	54	28	21	49	70

VINCENT LECAVALIER

Statistics– Club Team			Regular Season					Playoffs				
Season	Team	League	GP	G	A	PTS	PIM	GP	G	A	PTS	PIM
1996-97	RIM	QMJHL	64	42	61	103	38	4	4	3	7	2
1997-98	RIM	QMJHL	58	44	71	115	117	18	15	26	41	46
1998-99	TB	NHL	82	13	15	28	23	-	-	-	-	-
1999-00	TB	NHL	80	25	42	67	43	-	-	-	-	-
2000-01	TB	NHL	68	23	28	51	66	-	-	-	-	-
2001-02	TB	NHL	76	20	17	37	61	-	-	-	-	-
2002-03	TB	NHL	80	33	45	78	39	11	3	3	6	22
2003-04	TB	NHL	81	32	34	66	52	23	9	7	16	25
2004-05	KAZ	RUS	30	7	9	16	78	4	1	0	1	6
2005-06	TB	NHL	80	35	40	75	90	5	1	3	4	7
2006-07	TB	NHL	82	52	56	108	44	6	5	2	7	10
2007-08	TB	NHL	81	40	52	92	89	-	-	-	-	-
2008-09	TB	NHL	77	29	38	67	54	-	-	-	-	-
NHL CAREER			787	302	367	669	561	45	18	15	33	64

MILAN LUCIC

Statistics– Club Team

Season	Team	League	Regular Season					Playoffs				
			GP	G	A	PTS	PIM	GP	G	A	PTS	PIM
2004-05	VAN	WHL	1	0	0	0	2	2	0	0	0	0
2005-06	VAN	WHL	62	9	10	19	149	18	3	4	7	23
2006-07	VAN	WHL	70	30	38	68	147	22	7	12	19	26
2006-07	VAN	MemCup	-	-	-	-	-					
2007-08	BOS	NHL	77	8	19	27	89	7	2	0	2	4
2008-09	BOS	NHL	72	17	25	42	136	10	3	6	9	43
NHL CAREER			149	25	44	69	225	17	5	6	11	47

PATRICK MARLEAU

Statistics– Club Team

Season	Team	League	Regular Season					Playoffs				
			GP	G	A	PTS	PIM	GP	G	A	PTS	PIM
1995-96	SEA	WHL	72	32	42	74	22	5	3	4	7	4
1996-97	SEA	WHL	71	51	74	125	37	15	7	16	23	12
1997-98	SJ	NHL	74	13	19	32	14	5	0	1	1	0
1998-99	SJ	NHL	81	17	23	40	36	6	2	1	3	4
1999-00	SJ	NHL	81	21	24	45	24	5	1	1	2	2
2000-01	SJ	NHL	81	25	27	52	22	6	2	0	2	4
2001-02	SJ	NHL	79	21	23	44	40	12	6	5	11	6
2002-03	SJ	NHL	82	28	29	57	33	-	-	-	-	-
2003-04	SJ	NHL	80	28	29	57	24	17	8	4	12	6
2005-06	SJ	NHL	82	34	52	78	33	11	9	5	14	8
2006-07	SJ	NHL	77	32	46	78	33	11	3	3	6	2
2007-08	SJ	NHL	78	19	29	48	12	13	4	4	8	2
2008-09	SJ	NHL	76	38	33	71	18	6	2	1	3	8
NHL CAREER			971	276	334	610	303	92	37	25	62	42

ANDY MCDONALD

Statistics– Club Team			Regular Season					Playoffs				
Season	Team	League	GP	G	A	PTS	PIM	GP	G	A	PTS	PIM
1996-97	COL	ECAC	33	9	10	19	16					
1997-98	COL	ECAC	35	13	19	32	26					
1998-99	COL	ECAC	35	20	26	46	42					
1999-00	COL	ECAC	34	25	33	58	49					
2000-01	CIN	AHL	46	15	25	40	21	3	0	1	1	2
2000-01	ANA	NHL	16	1	0	1	6					
2001-02	CIN	AHL	21	7	25	32	6					
2001-02	ANA	NHL	53	7	21	28	10					
2002-03	ANA	NHL	46	10	11	21	14					
2003-04	ANA	NHL	79	9	21	30	24					
2004-05	ING	DEL	36	13	17	30	26	10	5	2	7	35
2005-06	ANA	NHL	82	34	51	85	32	16	2	7	9	10
2006-07	ANA	NHL	82	27	51	78	46	21	10	4	14	10
2007-08	STL	NHL	49	14	22	36	32	-	-	-	-	-
2008-09	STL	NHL	46	15	29	44	24	4	1	3	4	0
NHL CAREER			486	121	218	339	218	41	13	14	27	20

BRENDEN MORROW

Statistics– Club Team			Regular Season					Playoffs				
Season	Team	League	GP	G	A	PTS	PIM	GP	G	A	PTS	PIM
1995-96	PORT	WHL	65	13	12	25	61	7	0	0	0	8
1996-97	PORT	WHL	71	39	49	88	178	6	2	1	3	4
1997-98	PORT	WHL	68	34	52	86	184	16	10	8	18	65
1997-98	PORT	MemCup	-	-	-	-	-	4	1	2	3	20
1998-99	PORT	WHL	61	41	44	85	248	4	0	4	4	18
1999-00	MICH	IHL	9	2	0	2	18	-	-	-	-	-
1999-00	DAL	NHL	64	14	19	33	81	21	2	4	6	22
2000-01	DAL	NHL	82	20	24	44	128	10	0	3	3	12
2001-02	DAL	NHL	72	17	18	35	109	-	-	-	-	-
2002-03	DAL	NHL	71	21	22	43	134	12	3	5	8	16
2003-04	DAL	NHL	81	25	24	49	121	5	0	1	1	4
2004-05	O.C.	CHL	19	8	14	22	31	-	-	-	-	-
2005-06	DAL	NHL	81	23	42	65	183	5	1	5	6	6
2006-07	DAL	NHL	40	16	15	31	33	7	2	1	3	18
2007-08	DAL	NHL	82	32	42	74	105	18	9	6	15	22
2008-09	DAL	NHL	18	5	10	15	49	-	-	-	-	-
NHL CAREER			591	173	216	389	943	78	17	25	42	100

RICK NASH

Statistics– Club Team			Regular Season					Playoffs				
Season	Team	League	GP	G	A	PTS	PIM	GP	G	A	PTS	PIM
2000-01	LDN	OHL	58	31	35	66	56	4	3	3	6	8
2001-02	LDN	OHL	54	32	40	72	88	12	10	9	19	21
2002-03	CBJ	NHL	74	17	22	39	78	-	-	-	-	-
2003-04	CBJ	NHL	80	41	16	57	87	-	-	-	-	-
2004-05	DAV	SUI	44	26	20	46	83	15	9	2	11	26
2005-06	CBJ	NHL	54	31	23	54	51	-	-	-	-	-
2006-07	CBJ	NHL	75	27	30	57	73	-	-	-	-	-
2007-08	CBJ	NHL	80	38	31	69	95	-	-	-	-	-
2008-09	CBJ	NHL	78	49	39	79	52	4	1	2	3	2
NHL CAREER			441	194	161	355	436	4	1	2	3	2

COREY PERRY

Statistics– Club Team			Regular Season					Playoffs				
Season	Team	League	GP	G	A	PTS	PIM	GP	G	A	PTS	PIM
2001-02	LDN	OHL	67	28	31	59	56	12	2	3	5	30
2002-03	LDN	OHL	67	25	53	78	145	14	7	16	23	27
2003-04	LDN	OHL	66	40	73	224	98	15	7	15	22	20
2003-04	LDN	MemCup	-	-	-	-	-	4	4	3	7	5
2004-05	LDN	OHL	60	47	83	130	117	18	11	27	38	46
2004-05	CIN	AHL	-	-	-	-	-	3	1	1	2	4
2005-06	PORT	AHL	19	16	18	34	32	1	1	0	1	0
2005-06	ANA	NHL	56	13	12	25	50	11	0	3	3	16
2006-07	ANA	NHL	82	17	27	44	55	21	6	9	15	37
2007-08	ANA	NHL	70	29	25	54	108	3	2	1	3	8
2008-09	ANA	NHL	78	32	40	72	109	13	8	6	14	36
NHL CAREER			286	91	104	195	322	48	16	19	35	97

MICHAEL RICHARDS

Statistics– Club Team			Regular Season					Playoffs				
Season	Team	League	GP	G	A	PTS	PIM	GP	G	A	PTS	PIM
2001-02	KIT	OHL	65	20	38	58	52	4	0	1	1	6
2002-03	KIT	OHL	67	37	50	87	99	21	9	18	27	24
2002-03	KIT	MemCup	-	-	-	-	-					
2003-04	KIT	OHL	58	36	53	89	82	1	0	0	0	0
2004-05	KIT	OHL	43	22	36	58	75	15	11	17	28	36
2004-05	PHI	AHL	-	-	-	-	-	14	7	8	15	28
2005-06	PHI	NHL	79	11	23	34	65	6	0	1	1	0
2006-07	PHI	NHL	59	10	22	32	52	-	-	-	-	-
2007-08	PHI	NHL	73	28	47	75	76	17	7	7	14	10
2008-09	PHI	NHL	79	30	50	80	63	6	1	4	5	6
NHL CAREER			290	79	142	221	256	29	8	12	20	16

DEREK ROY

Statistics– Club Team			Regular Season					Playoffs				
Season	Team	League	GP	G	A	PTS	PIM	GP	G	A	PTS	PIM
1999-00	KIT	OHL	66	34	53	87	44	5	4	1	5	6
2000-01	KIT	OHL	65	42	39	71	114	-	-	-	-	-
2001-02	KIT	OHL	62	43	46	89	92	4	1	2	3	2
2002-03	KIT	OHL	49	28	50	78	73	21	9	23	32	14
2002-03	KIT	MemCup	-	-	-	-	-					
2003-04	ROCH	AHL	26	10	16	26	20	16	6	8	14	18
2003-04	BUF	NHL	49	9	10	19	12	-	-	-	-	-
2004-05	ROCH	AHL	67	16	45	61	10	9	6	5	11	6
2005-06	ROCH	AHL	8	7	13	20	10	-	-	-	-	-
2005-06	BUF	NHL	70	18	28	46	57	18	5	10	15	16
2006-07	BUF	NHL	75	21	42	63	60	16	2	5	7	14
2007-08	BUF	NHL	78	32	49	81	46	-	-	-	-	-
2008-09	BUF	NHL	82	28	42	70	38	-	-	-	-	-
NHL CAREER			354	108	171	279	213	34	7	15	22	30

PATRICK SHARP

Statistics– Club Team			Regular Season					Playoffs				
Season	Team	League	GP	G	A	PTS	PIM	GP	G	A	PTS	PIM
2000-01	VERM	ECAC	34	12	15	27	36	-	-	-	-	-
2001-02	VERM	ECAC	31	13	13	26	50	-	-	-	-	-
2002-03	PHA	AHL	53	14	19	33	39	-	-	-	-	-
2002-03	PHA	NHL	3	0	0	0	2	-	-	-	-	-
2003-04	PHA	AHL	35	15	14	29	45	1	2	0	2	0
2003-04	PHA	NHL	41	5	2	7	55	12	1	0	1	2
2004-05	PHA	AHL	75	23	29	52	08	21	8	13	21	20
2005-06	CHI	NHL	72	14	17	31	46	-	-	-	-	-
2006-07	CHI	NHL	80	20	15	35	74	-	-	-	-	-
2007-08	CHI	NHL	80	36	26	62	55	-	-	-	-	-
2008-09	CHI	NHL	61	26	18	44	41	17	7	4	11	6
NHL CAREER			337	101	78	179	273	29	8	4	12	8

RYAN SMYTH

Statistics– Club Team

Season	Team	League	Regular Season					Playoffs				
			GP	G	A	PTS	PIM	GP	G	A	PTS	PIM
1991-92	M.J.	WHL	2	0	0	0	0	-	-	-	-	-
1992-93	M.J.	WHL	64	19	14	33	59	-	-	-	-	-
1993-94	M.J.	WHL	72	50	55	105	88	-	-	-	-	-
1994-95	EDM	NHL	3	0	0	0	0	-	-	-	-	-
1994-95	M.J.	WHL	50	51	45	86	66	10	6	9	15	22
1995-96	C.B.	AHL	9	6	5	11	4	-	-	-	-	-
1995-96	EDM	NHL	48	2	9	11	28	-	-	-	-	-
1996-97	EDM	NHL	82	39	22	61	76	12	5	5	10	12
1997-98	EDM	NHL	65	20	13	33	44	12	1	3	4	16
1998-99	EDM	NHL	71	13	18	31	62	3	3	0	3	0
1999-00	EDM	NHL	82	28	26	54	58	5	1	0	1	6
2000-01	EDM	NHL	82	31	39	70	58	6	3	4	7	4
2001-02	EDM	NHL	61	15	35	50	48	-	-	-	-	-
2002-03	EDM	NHL	66	27	34	61	67	6	2	0	2	16
2003-04	EDM	NHL	82	23	36	59	70	-	-	-	-	-
2005-06	EDM	NHL	75	36	30	66	58	24	7	9	16	22
2006-07	NYI	NHL	71	36	32	68	52	5	1	3	4	4
2007-08	COL	NHL	55	14	23	37	50	8	2	3	5	2
2008-09	COL	NHL	77	26	33	59	62	-	-	-	-	-
NHL CAREER			920	310	350	660	733	81	25	27	52	82

JASON SPEZZA

Statistics– Club Team

Season	Team	League	Regular Season					Playoffs				
			GP	G	A	PTS	PIM	GP	G	A	PTS	PIM
1998-99	BRM	OHL	67	22	49	71	18	-	-	-	-	-
1999-00	MISS	OHL	52	24	37	61	33	-	-	-	-	-
2000-01	WND	OHL	56	43	73	116	43	9	4	5	9	10
2001-02	BEL	OHL	53	42	63	105	42	-	-	-	-	-
2001-02	G.R.	AHL	-	-	-	-	-	3	1	0	1	2
2002-03	BING	AHL	43	22	32	54	71	2	1	2	3	4
2002-03	OTT	NHL	33	7	14	21	8	3	1	1	2	0
2003-04	OTT	NHL	78	22	33	55	71	3	0	0	0	2
2004-05	BING	AHL	80	32	85	117	50	6	1	3	4	6
2005-06	OTT	NHL	68	19	71	90	33	10	5	9	14	2
2006-07	OTT	NHL	67	34	53	87	45	20	7	15	22	10
2007-08	OTT	NHL	76	34	58	92	66	4	0	1	1	0
2008-09	OTT	NHL	82	32	41	73	79	-	-	-	-	-
NHL CAREER			404	148	270	418	302	40	13	26	39	14

MARTIN ST. LOUIS

Statistics– Club Team			Regular Season					Playoffs				
Season	Team	League	GP	G	A	PTS	PIM	GP	G	A	PTS	PIM
1993-94	VERM	ECAC	33	15	36	51	24	-	-	-	-	-
1994-95	VERM	ECAC	35	23	48	71	36	-	-	-	-	-
1995-96	VERM	ECAC	35	29	56	85	38	-	-	-	-	-
1996-97	VERM	ECAC	36	24	36	60	65	-	-	-	-	-
1997-98	CLE	IHL	56	16	34	50	24	-	-	-	-	-
1997-98	STJ	AHL	25	15	11	26	20	20	5	15	20	16
1998-99	STJ	AHL	53	28	34	62	30	7	4	4	8	2
1998-99	CGY	NHL	13	1	1	2	10	-	-	-	-	-
1999-00	STJ	AHL	17	15	11	26	14	-	-	-	-	-
1999-00	CGY	NHL	56	3	15	18	22	-	-	-	-	-
2000-01	TB	NHL	78	18	22	40	12	-	-	-	-	-
2001-02	TB	NHL	53	16	19	35	20	-	-	-	-	-
2002-03	TB	NHL	82	33	37	70	32	11	7	5	12	0
2003-04	TB	NHL	82	38	56	94	24	23	9	15	24	14
2004-05	LAU	SUI	23	9	16	25	16	-	-	-	-	-
2005-06	TB	NHL	80	31	30	61	38	5	4	0	4	2
2006-07	TB	NHL	82	43	59	102	28	6	3	5	8	8
2007-08	TB	NHL	82	25	58	83	26	-	-	-	-	-
2008-09	TB	NHL	82	30	50	80	14	-	-	-	-	-
NHL CAREER			690	238	347	585	226	45	23	25	48	24

ERIC STAAL

Statistics– Club Team			Regular Season					Playoffs				
Season	Team	League	GP	G	A	PTS	PIM	GP	G	A	PTS	PIM
2000-01	PBO	OHL	63	19	30	49	23	7	2	5	7	4
2001-02	PBO	OHL	56	23	39	62	40	6	3	6	9	10
2002-03	PBO	OHL	66	39	59	98	36	7	9	5	14	6
2003-04	CAR	NHL	81	11	20	31	40	-	-	-	-	-
2004-05	LOW	AHL	77	26	51	77	88	11	2	8	10	12
2005-06	CAR	NHL	82	45	55	100	81	25	9	19	28	8
2006-07	CAR	NHL	82	30	40	70	68					
2007-08	CAR	NHL	82	38	44	82	50					
2008-09	CAR	NHL	82	40	35	75	50	18	10	5	15	4
NHL CAREER			409	164	194	358	289	43	19	24	43	12

JORDAN STAAL

Statistics– Club Team			Regular Season					Playoffs				
Season	Team	League	GP	G	A	PTS	PIM	GP	G	A	PTS	PIM
2004-05	PBO	OHL	66	9	19	28	29	14	5	5	10	16
2005-06	PBO	OHL	68	28	40	68	69	19	10	6	16	16
2006-07	PIT	NHL	81	29	13	42	24	5	3	0	3	2
2007-08	PIT	NHL	82	12	16	28	55	20	6	1	7	14
2008-09	PIT	NHL	82	22	27	49	37	24	4	5	9	8
NHL CAREER			245	63	56	119	116	49	13	6	19	24

JOE THORNTON

Statistics– Club Team			Regular Season					Playoffs				
Season	Team	League	GP	G	A	PTS	PIM	GP	G	A	PTS	PIM
1995-96	SSM	OHL	66	30	46	76	51	4	1	1	2	11
1996-97	SSM	OHL	59	41	81	122	123	11	11	8	19	24
1997-98	BOS	NHL	55	3	4	7	19	6	0	0	0	9
1998-99	BOS	NHL	81	16	25	41	69	11	3	6	9	4
1999-00	BOS	NHL	81	23	37	60	82	-	-	-	-	-
2000-01	BOS	NHL	72	37	34	71	107	-	-	-	-	-
2001-02	BOS	NHL	66	22	46	68	127	6	2	4	6	10
2002-03	BOS	NHL	77	36	65	101	109	5	1	2	3	4
2003-04	BOS	NHL	77	23	50	73	98	7	0	0	0	14
2004-05	DAV	SUI	40	10	44	54	80	14	4	20	24	29
2005-06	SJ	NHL	81	29	96	125	61	11	2	7	9	12
2006-07	SJ	NHL	82	22	92	114	44	11	1	10	11	10
2007-08	SJ	NHL	82	29	67	96	59	13	2	8	10	2
2008-09	SJ	NHL	82	25	61	86	56	6	1	4	5	5
NHL CAREER			836	265	577	842	831	76	12	41	53	70

JONATHAN TOEWS

Statistics– Club Team			Regular Season					Playoffs				
Season	Team	League	GP	G	A	PTS	PIM	GP	G	A	PTS	PIM
2005-06	UND	WCHA	42	22	17	39	22	5	2	3	5	-
2005-06	UND	NCAA Champ	-	-	-	-	-	3	3	3	6	-
2006-07	UND	WCHA	34	18	28	46	10	4	3	2	5	-
2006-07	UND	NCAA Champ	-	-	-	-	-	3	2	1	3	-
2007-08	CHI	NHL	64	24	30	54	44	-	-	-	-	-
2008-09	CHI	NHL	82	34	35	69	51	17	7	6	13	26
NHL CAREER			146	58	65	123	95	17	7	6	13	26

GAME SHEETS

<table>
<tr><td colspan="2">Game One</td><td colspan="4" rowspan="4"></td></tr>
<tr><td>Preliminary Round</td><td>Canada _____ vs. Norway _____</td></tr>
<tr><td align="right">Date:</td><td>Thursday February 16th, 2010   16:30</td></tr>
<tr><td align="right">Venue:</td><td>Canada Hockey Place</td></tr>
<tr><td>Player Number</td><td>Player Name</td><td>Goals</td><td>Assists</td><td>Points</td><td>PIM</td></tr>
<tr><td></td><td></td><td></td><td></td><td></td><td></td></tr>
<tr><td></td><td></td><td></td><td></td><td></td><td></td></tr>
<tr><td></td><td></td><td></td><td></td><td></td><td></td></tr>
<tr><td></td><td></td><td></td><td></td><td></td><td></td></tr>
<tr><td></td><td></td><td></td><td></td><td></td><td></td></tr>
<tr><td></td><td></td><td></td><td></td><td></td><td></td></tr>
<tr><td></td><td></td><td></td><td></td><td></td><td></td></tr>
<tr><td></td><td></td><td></td><td></td><td></td><td></td></tr>
<tr><td></td><td></td><td></td><td></td><td></td><td></td></tr>
<tr><td></td><td></td><td></td><td></td><td></td><td></td></tr>
<tr><td></td><td></td><td></td><td></td><td></td><td></td></tr>
<tr><td></td><td></td><td></td><td></td><td></td><td></td></tr>
<tr><td></td><td></td><td></td><td></td><td></td><td></td></tr>
<tr><td></td><td></td><td></td><td></td><td></td><td></td></tr>
<tr><td></td><td></td><td></td><td></td><td></td><td></td></tr>
<tr><td></td><td></td><td></td><td></td><td></td><td></td></tr>
<tr><td></td><td></td><td></td><td></td><td></td><td></td></tr>
<tr><td></td><td></td><td></td><td></td><td></td><td></td></tr>
<tr><td></td><td></td><td></td><td></td><td></td><td></td></tr>
<tr><td></td><td></td><td></td><td></td><td></td><td></td></tr>
<tr><td>Goalies</td><td>Player Name</td><td>G.A.</td><td>S.A.</td><td>Avg.</td><td>Mins.</td><td>PIM</td></tr>
<tr><td></td><td></td><td></td><td></td><td></td><td></td><td></td></tr>
<tr><td></td><td></td><td></td><td></td><td></td><td></td><td></td></tr>
<tr><td></td><td></td><td></td><td></td><td></td><td></td><td></td></tr>
</table>

Game Two

Preliminary Round	Canada _____ vs. Switzerland _____				
Date:	Thursday February 18th 2010 16:30				
Venue:	Canada Hockey Place				

Player Number	Player Name	Goals	Assists	Points	PIM

Goalies	Player Name	G.A.	S.A.	Avg.	Mins.	PIM

Game Three

Preliminary Round	Canada _____ vs. U.S.A. _____
Date:	Sunday, February 21st 2010 16:40
Venue:	Canada Hockey Place

CANADA

Player Number	Player Name	Goals	Assists	Points	PIM

Goalies	Player Name	G.A.	S.A.	Avg.	Mins.	PIM

Game Four (if necessary– see page 224)

Qualification Round	Canada _____ vs. _____				
Date:	Tuesday, February 23rd 2010　　16:30				
Venue:					

Player Number	Player Name	Goals	Assists	Points	PIM

Goalies	Player Name	G.A.	S.A.	Avg.	Mins.	PIM

Game Five

Quarter-Final	_____ vs. _____
Date:	Wednesday, February 24th 2010 16:30
Venue:	

CANADA

Player Number	Player Name	Goals	Assists	Points	PIM

Goalies	Player Name	G.A.	S.A.	Avg.	Mins.	PIM

Game Six

Semifinal	_____ vs. _____
Date:	Friday, February 26th 2010 18:30
Venue:	Canada Hockey Place

CANADA

Player Number	Player Name	Goals	Assists	Points	PIM

Goalies	Player Name	G.A.	S.A.	Avg.	Mins.	PIM

Game Seven					
Bronze	_____ vs. _____				
Date:	Saturday, February 27th 2010 19:00				
Venue:	Canada Hockey Place				

Player Number	Player Name	Goals	Assists	Points	PIM

Goalies	Player Name	G.A.	S.A.	Avg.	Mins.	PIM

Game Eight

			Goals	Assists	Points	PIM
Gold	_____ vs. _____					
Date:	Sunday, February 28th 2010 12:15					
Venue:	Canada Hockey Place					

Player Number	Player Name	Goals	Assists	Points	PIM

Goalies	Player Name	G.A.	S.A.	Avg.	Mins.	PIM

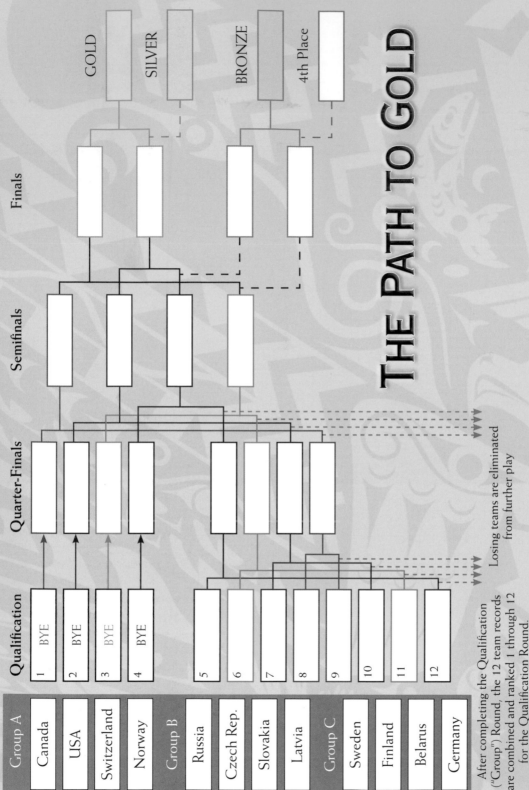

THE PATH TO GOLD

Qualification — Quarter-Finals — Semifinals — Finals

GOLD
SILVER
BRONZE
4th Place

Group A		
Canada	1	BYE
USA	2	BYE
Switzerland	3	BYE
Norway	4	BYE

Group B		
Russia	5	
Czech Rep.	6	
Slovakia	7	
Latvia	8	

Group C		
Sweden	9	
Finland	10	
Belarus	11	
Germany	12	

Losing teams are eliminated from further play

After completing the Qualification ("Group") Round, the 12 team records are combined and ranked 1 through 12 for the Qualification Round. The top 4 teams receive a "bye," and proceed directly to the Quarter-Finals.